B&T
$7.95
JAN 11 '78

W9-CCY-661

PUBLIC
PERSONS

PUBLIC
PERSONS

Walter Lippmann

Edited by
Gilbert A. Harrison

LIVERIGHT  NEW YORK

Wingate College Library

Copyright © 1976 by Liveright Publishing Corporation. All rights reserved.
Published simultaneously in Canada by George J. McLeod Limited, Toronto.
Printed in the United States of America.

First Edition

Library of Congress Cataloging in Publication Data
Lippmann, Walter, 1889–1974.
    Public persons.
    1. United States—Biography.   I. Title.
CT220.L56   1976   920'.073   76–23103
ISBN 0–87140–620–9

1 2 3 4 5 6 7 8 9 0

Contents

5

072138

Acknowledgment

Walter Lippmann was fortunate in having, not a Boswell, but a devoted former telephone company official, Robert O. Anthony, who for more than forty years collected every bit of writing by or about Lippmann that he could get his hands on. He was not paid to do it. He had not met Lippmann when he began. It is he who was responsible for classifying some 150,000 Lippmann papers deposited at Yale University's Sterling Library, and this collection of essays was assembled with his help.

G.A.H.

PUBLIC
PERSONS

Introduction

Walter Lippmann's work so fulfilled his talents that it is hard to imagine his having been anything but what he was, the model political journalist, successful from the start. He was "the most brilliant man of his age in all the United States," in the opinion of Theodore Roosevelt; "mature at twenty-three, when most of us were floundering about in a prolonged adolescence," according to his Harvard contemporary Van Wyck Brooks. Even his *New Republic* colleague, Francis Hackett, whose romanticism ran counter to Lippmann's realism, had to say that he was "wide-awake at the age of twenty-four . . . up bright and early like the sun in the South."

Born September 23, 1889 in New York City where he died December 14, 1974, Lippmann was the only child of prosperous German Jewish parents. He attended a select boys' academy, Sachs Institute, and at thirteen wrote his first published article for the school *Record,* a mournful description of an Italian convict being led to his execution. At Harvard, completing the four-year course in three years and graduating Phi Beta Kappa in 1910, Lippmann joined the socialist club, an infatuation that lasted only a few years. He studied under Graham Wallas, whose thought marked him permanently. Wallas' book, *The Great Society,* was dedicated to Lippmann.

Had he chosen an academic career, Lippmann would have done well at it. He read widely, he was articulate, he enjoyed the play of ideas. But classroom teaching seems never to have occurred to him and would probably not have satisfied his more worldly tastes. He wanted to be in the swim, and he was. He wanted lively company, including the company of the eminent, and he had it. He was acquainted with every President from Theodore Roosevelt to Richard Nixon, and in the 1920s traveled once a week by train

11

from New York to Washington for lunch at the White House with Calvin Coolidge—a "loquacious" man, he reported, not profoundly troubled by the troubles of others. He vacationed with the Lamonts, visited Bernard Berenson in Italy, was the guest of Khrushchev on the Black Sea, and was welcome at the Elysée Palace in Paris. Statesmen sought and were given his counsel, though Lippmann firmly insisted that "a certain distance" be kept between public officials and newspapermen—"not a wall or fence, but an air space."

His schedule, one admirer remarked, was "worked through with the regularity of a railroad; he gets more done in a day than the whole population of England." Lippmann worked wherever he was—Bar Harbor, Maine in the summer, Europe in the spring, and New York or Washington the rest of the year. Idleness bored him, and the thought of retirement appalled him. Throughout his life what he did, essentially, was to study and describe how we are governed and how we might be better governed, and for half a century a large number of Americans did not know what they thought about those questions until Lippmann told them.

He never learned to type. His articles were written in a small, nearly illegible script, and in later years were read into a dictating machine and transcribed. They were sometimes revised extensively and sometimes barely touched, depending on the complexity of the subject and his familiarity with it. Whatever the subject, he had his theme clearly in mind before pen was put to paper.

With the morning's reading and writing done, Lippmann dressed for lunch, usually at the Metropolitan Club in Washington or the Century Club in New York, and always preceded by a cocktail. His guest had the full attention of a gifted listener, for Lippmann was "probably the only newspaperman of his time," as Philip Geyelin of *The Washington Post* has recalled, "who could get away with sitting back after the preliminary courtesies with a foreign minister or head of state, folding his arms and simply saying nothing. . . . The effect on some of the strongest of his subjects was to make them blurt out their innermost confidences in a desperate effort to fill the void."

After lunch, Lippmann rested, played golf with his wife Helen (croquet or tennis if they were at Bar Harbor), walked their large black poodle, or went to a movie. This was followed by a dinner party from which the Lippmanns departed when Walter had heard all he cared to hear, which could be quite early.

At its peak, his column "Today and Tomorrow" reached 13 million readers and was the most influential political commentary in the country. It was not used as a platform for exhortation. Instead, in a dispassionate tone, the column explained what was happening in Washington or in some other world capital, why it was happening, and where a given policy was likely to lead. Confidences were respected, and unless he was reporting a lengthy interview with someone like Charles de Gaulle, he did not reveal what prominent personages had told him.

Although numerous in the 1920s and 1930s, his outside articles and speeches were rarities by the 1960s, by which time he had a rule against accepting any honorary degree that required his delivering an address.

Lippmann shrewdly assessed the value of his reputation; it was not to be squandered on trivial topics or audiences, or lost causes. Nor, to the disappointment of more partisan-minded friends, would he allow his personal preferences to determine his public judgments. Many hoped he would support the presidential candidacies of Adlai Stevenson in 1952 and Eugene McCarthy in 1968 —were they not, after all, his sort of men, thoughtful and urbane? They were, but Lippmann endorsed their Republican opponents. He did so in the first instance because he believed that General Eisenhower would make the Republican party responsible, and would quickly end the war in Korea without domestic recriminations; in the second instance he believed that Richard Nixon would do the same in Indochina. He was fifty percent right. He did not apologize for being wrong, assuming that his readers understood that he was writing to pressing deadlines, and in the light of information then at hand.

Punditry is a risky vocation, and Lippmann was faulted for an occasional misjudgment but he was never faulted for his handling of the English language. The prose was like flypaper; "if I touch it," Justice Holmes said, "I am stuck till I finish it." One had to read to the end of an essay that began: "If an optimist is a man who makes lemonade out of all the lemons that are handed him, then Senator Harding is the greatest of all optimists."

From Harvard, Lippmann had gone straight into journalism.

13

Wingate College Library

He worked briefly on *The Boston Common* and for a year with Lincoln Steffens on *Everybody's Magazine,* which he left to write his first book, *A Preface to Politics* (1913). The following year, he joined the staff Herbert Croly was assembling for a new weekly journal of opinion, *The New Republic.* In its pages he roamed widely, discussing Army intelligence tests, John D. Rockefeller, tennis matches, Jung, Woodrow Wilson, and how the American press covered the Russian Revolution ("nothing short of a disaster").

There was a bravado, a sardonic wit, an informality in those early pieces that Lippmann later repressed. "Ever since Miss Amy Lowell explained the 'new manner' in poetry," he wrote in 1916, "I have been trying to imagine life lived as she describes it. For she says that there has been a changed attitude towards life which compel a poet to paint landscapes because they are beautiful and not because they suit his moods, to tell stories because they are interesting and not because they prove a thesis. I don't understand this 'externality'; I don't know what it means to be interested in 'things for themselves.' "

Explaining why the fashion for utopias had passed, he said they read "like the epilogue for little Eva in heaven spread out into a five-act play. They are the happy endings of a drama which the author was unable to write. They give the result which is obvious and shirk the process which is difficult . . . . One of the loveliest utopias I ever knew was of sunburnt philosophers playing with shells on a coral island written by a friend of mine living in Washington Square who wished he could spend the winter in Bermuda. It filled him with passionate revolt to think that Manhattan was not a coral island peopled with the lithe, brown naked bodies of laughing philosophers. Well, it filled him with revolt, and left Manhattan otherwise unchanged."

Shortly after the United States entered World War I, Lippmann went to France as a captain in military intelligence. He served on Colonel House's staff during the Paris peace negotiations and helped draft President Wilson's Fourteen Points. It was a heady experience for a journalist who had just turned thirty, and a sobering one. "As soon as the terms of the settlement were known," Lippmann recalled long afterwards, "it was evident that peace had not been made with Germany. . . . Public opinion, having vetoed reconciliation, had made the settlement unworkable." He returned from France convinced that the punitive victors had sown dragon's teeth, and he came to think that "mass opinion" in the liberal democracies was largely to blame for that failure; it had acquired "mounting power" and shown itself to be "a dangerous master of decisions when the stakes are life and death."

Back on *The New Republic,* Lippmann shared his colleagues' admiration for the League of Nations, and their opposition to imposing harsh reparations payments on the defeated Germans. The United States Senate did not agree.

In 1922, Lippmann found a larger audience on Joseph Pulitzer's New York *World,* whose editorial page he ran from 1924 until the newspaper folded in 1931. It was the best page of its era, and Lippmann liked the anonymity of the editorial "we." Then came the invitation of Ogden and Helen Reid to write a signed, syndicated column for *The Herald-Tribune,* which Lippmann accepted.

Asked to state his business he would answer, "newspaperman," a label he wore proudly but distinctively, for he was not in the least like the hardbitten, hard-drinking newspaperman dramatized by Hecht and MacArthur in *The Front Page.* Scooping one's rivals or busting city hall did not interest him; he was after the big story, the story of shifting tides that carry societies to shipwreck or safety. "The function of the news," he wrote in *Public Opinion* (1922), "is to signalize an event, the function of truth is to bring to light hidden facts, and to set them in relation with other facts, and to make a picture of reality on which men can act." That a majority did not always see the picture Lippmann saw or always act wisely, did not divert him from his task. The world would go on best, he told the Phi Beta Kappa chapter at Columbia in 1932, "if among us there are men who have stood apart, who refused to be anxious or too much concerned, who were cool and inquiring, and had their eyes on a larger past and a longer future."

There were two Lippmanns. The columnist was attentive to the day's news; the writer of books was on the lookout for clues to tomorrow. The newspaperman wrote about unemployment and the latest pronouncement of the Secretary of State; the philosopher reflected on the nature of freedom and the dangers of uninhibited popular rule.

This philosophical side of Lippmann had been stimulated at Harvard by an extraordinary group of teachers—Graham Wallas, William James, Irving Babbitt, George Santayana, Josiah Royce —and traces of their thought run though his work. From James he learned that "the essence of life is its continually changing character," which Lippmann translated to mean that "it is a mistake to think that we could wear the same coat all the time, and a mistake to throw it away, supposing in the summer that it will never be winter again." Royce's definition of a reasonable man could have been written by Lippmann—one "capable of synopsis, of viewing both sides or many sides of a question, of comparing various motives, of taking interest in a totality rather than in a scattered multiplicity. . . . Reason, from this point of view, is the power to see widely and steadily and connectedly."

But the primacy of reason as a guide to conduct raised problems for Lippmann. The rub was the "inherent difficulty about using the method of reason to deal with an unreasoning world," and the fact that "the number of human problems on which reason is prepared to dictate is small." Yet if we are not governed by reason, how are we to be governed? How can we hold together? By what alchemy can selfish interests be dissolved into an elevating common allegiance? Again and again Lippmann returned to those questions and found a partial answer in leadership—a commanding personality who rallied the public to its larger, truer interests—someone like de Gaulle who saw "absolutely perfectly what's in the distance." Professional Babbitt had said that "societies always decay from the top." Well then, societies could be braced and fortified from the top and thus saved from the short-sightedness of the masses, who, Lippmann said, "cannot be counted on to apprehend regularly and promptly the reality of things."

Unhappily, except for de Gaulle and possibly Winston Churchill, the leaders of Lippmann's generation let him down, and he was finally, dismally, to say that the last great American President was James Madison. Theodore Roosevelt, Woodrow Wilson, Franklin Roosevelt, Lyndon Johnson, John Kennedy all at first gave off what Lippmann called a "warm aura of possibilities." But in each case, the aura faded, and then . . . then one had to wait for another to come forward and restrain the divisive and destructive impulses of the public, so that we could live, as he wrote in *The Phantom Public,* "free of the trampling and the roar of a bewildered herd."

If Lippmann paid little homage to the innate wisdom of the people, he nevertheless had "no wish to disenfranchise my fellow citizens"; noses had to be counted, whatever their shape. His point was that liberty and democracy require government that will,

16

when necessary, "swim against the tides of private feelings." Because the public is too divided, too poorly informed, and too self-regarding, authority had to be delegated, perhaps to "intelligence bureaus," or at least to those who are wiser than the many and who have the power to decide vexing questions on their own merits.

Since Lippmann was not a utopian and knew that in the real world we cannot expect to be ruled by philosopher-kings, he was ready to settle for less. He was not ready to settle for politicians who get ahead "only as they placate, appease, bribe, seduce, bamboozle and otherwise manage to manipulate demanding and threatening elements in their constituencies." But it was the seducers and bamboozlers who were generally in charge. And because they were in charge, an age that was "rich with varied and generous passions" had become disorderly and deranged; there were no twentieth-century heirs in America to the gentlemen from Virginia. We had lost "vital contact with the traditions of civility" as understood by Edmund Burke. And so Lippmann slowly turned, in the words of Benjamin F. Wright, to a "nostalgic defense of the glories of free trade, civility and natural law as they were accepted in the eighteenth century."

Little of this deepening pessimism was apparent in Lippmann's temperate columns. Although he was extremely troubled by the war in Indochina and felt that he had been misled by President Johnson, who had asked for and not accepted his opinion, he wrote about Johnson with no bitterness. When someone asked what he did with his anger, he replied, "I sit on it." He could not be censorious in print and did not need to prove how deftly he could take the skin off public officials. Knowing they would not be skinned, the officials were the readier to talk with him. In private, his customary response to the mention of an objectionable politician was a shrug, a wave of the hand, and a dismissive, "Oh, him." He would discredit the policies, but not the practitioners. On the infrequent occasions when Lippmann did write about personalities he made a portrait of ideas, meager in visual details and free of gossip. Only in his appreciative obituaries did his natural warmth come to the surface.

It was no use asking Lippmann to wrestle his opponents and pin them to the mat. Anyone who tried to persuade him to get tough soon gave up. Felix Frankfurter, whom he had known since the days they both wrote for *The New Republic,* accused him sitting in a noise-proof room and drafting things on paper, whereas, in Frankfurter's opinion, Lippmann should have gone through "the heartbreak of making paper walk." The estrangement of the two men had a history. Frankfurter was put off by Lippmann's imperviousness to advice. He may also have been made uncomfortable by Lippmann's strictures against presidential courtiers. He was certainly annoyed by a column in 1933 which he considered insufficiently alarmist about Hitler. And he could not have forgotten Lippmann's remark in 1932 that Franklin D. Roosevelt, Frankfurter's idol, was "no enemy of entrenched privilege" and had "no important qualifications for the Presidency."

Mabel Dodge, whose radical "Evenings" in her New York apartment the twenty-four-year-old Lippmann had attended, wrote that, "Walter will never, never lose an eye in a fight," and others said that he pulled his punches. He did, but not because he was afraid of being hurt, Restraint was as intrinsic to him as he believed civility is to a well-ordered community. If "decorum is the supreme virtue of the humanist," as Professor Babbitt thought, for Lippmann, decorum reflected a deference to life's ambiguities and to the necessity of practical human accommodation. He not only appreciated a point of view with which he differed, he stated it better than its proponent. And he did it deliberately. "Whenever men are bent on persuading and influencing other men," he wrote, "some prudence in respect to their prejudices is necessary to success." When one is clear about that, "he is in no danger of confusing his timidity, his convenience, and his ambition with a just prudence."

The outward Lippmann was convivial, amusing, and self-assured. Few knew how he struggled until a year before his death at eighty-five to make the themes in his *The Public Philosophy* clearer. In that last book, he had tried to account for the decline of Western democracies and prescribe for their revival. He had concluded that the constitutional order could not stand on a "quagmire of moral impressionism"; it needed a firmer foundation. But it *is* possible, he said, to discover by rational inquiry "the conditions which must be met if there is to be a good society." Democracies would continue to be demoralized and unmanageable until their citizens discerned a realm of being which is "sovereign above the infinite number of contradictory and competing private worlds"—

18

a realm of being that exists not because we will to believe it, as William James might have said; and not because our souls have an "invincible surmise" that it is there, as Josiah Royce thought; and not because one chooses to invent it, as Jean Paul Sartre would have it. This transcendent realm is real, Lippmann wrote; it rests on "hard intellectual ground," and it must have and hold men's highest loyalties. On that ground, democracies could defend themselves against the Jacobins of the modern world, who "war against freedom, against justice, against the laws and against the order of the good society."

Those ideas in *The Public Philosophy* were light years from the cheerier make-do's and can-do's of Lippmann's earlier *Preface to Politics* or *The Preface to Morals,* but they did not finally satisfy their author. He saw that the tension between a man's private impulses and transcendent truth was the "inexhaustible theme of human discourse," and that the "occasional harmonies in the lives of saints and the deeds of heroes and the excellence of genius are his glory." But glory was the exception, wretchedness the rule. "The decline of the power and influence and self-confidence of the western democracies" had been steep and sudden; we had "fallen far in a short span of time."

Rational inquiry had brought Lippmann to the edge of mystery, and to the edge of despair. For he was not one, in Wordsworth's phrase, "in whom persuasion and belief had ripened into faith, and faith become a passionate intuition."

Gilbert A. Harrison

19

William James

Within a week of the death of Professor William James of Harvard University, the newspapers had it that Mr. M. S. Ayer of Boston had received a message from his spirit. This news item provoked the ridicule of the people who don't believe in ghosts, but the joke was on Mr. Ayer of Boston. When, however, it was reported that Professor James himself had agreed to communicate with this world, if he could, and, in order to test the reports, had left a sealed message to be opened at a certain definite time after his death, the incredulous gasped at the professor's amazing "credulity."

William James wasn't "credulous." He was simply open-minded. Maybe the soul of man *is* immortal. The professors couldn't prove it wasn't, so James was willing to open his mind to evidence. He was willing to hunt for evidence, and to be convinced by it.

And in that he was simply keeping America's promise: he was actually doing what we, as a nation, proclaimed that we would do. He was tolerant; he was willing to listen to what seems preposterous, and to consider what might, though queer, be true. And he showed that this democratic attitude of mind is every bit as fruitful as the aristocratic determination to ignore new and strange-looking ideas. James was a democrat. He gave all men and all creeds, any idea, any theory, any superstition, a respectful hearing.

His interest in spiritualism is merely one illustration in a thousand. The hard scientists knew it was a hoax because they couldn't explain it, and the sentimentalists knew it was the truth because they wished it to be: but James wanted to know the facts. So he went to Mrs. Piper, and heard her out. Nay, he listened to Palladino and to Münsterberg. They pretended to know, and maybe they did.

And last year, when Frank Harris published his book on Shakespeare, to show that the "unknown" life and character of the poet could be drawn from his works, the other professors laughed the theory out of court. James went to Shakespeare and read the plays all over again to test the Harris theory. Maybe the poet *could* be known by his works. The fact that the theory was revolutionary did not alter the possibility that it might be true.

So with religion. A scientist, living in an age when science is dogmatically irreligious, he turned from its cocksure reasoning to ask for the facts. He went to the lives of the saints! Not to Herbert Spencer, you see. When he wanted to study the religious experience he went to the people who had had it, to Santa Theresa and Mrs. Eddy. They might know something the professors didn't know.

And again: at the age of sixty-five, with the whole of New England's individualism behind him, he asked about socialism. When he met H. G. Wells, he listened to the socialist, and, as it happens, was converted. So he said so. James was no more afraid of a new political theory than he was of ghosts, and he was no more afraid of proclaiming a new theory, or an old one, than he was of being a ghost. I think he would have listened with an open mind to the devil's account of heaven, and I'm sure he would have heard him out on hell.

James knew that he didn't know. He never acted upon the notion that the truth was his store of wisdom. Perhaps that is why he kept on rummaging about in other people's stores, and commending their goods. He seemed to take a delight in writing introductions, and appreciations of new books, and in going out of his way to listen to a young doctor of philosophy, or an undergraduate discussion of pragmatism, or the poetry of an obscure mystic. And, optimist that he was, by virtue of his unceasing freshness of interest, there is nothing more open-minded in our literature than his chivalrous respect for the pessimism of Francis Thompson.

> Speak not of comfort where no comfort is,
> Speak not at all: can words make foul things fair?
> Our life's a cheat, our death a black abyss:
> Hush and be mute, envisaging despair.

He felt with all sorts of men. He understood their demand for immediate answers to the great speculative questions of life. God, freedom, immortality, nature as moral or non-moral—these were for him not matters of idle scientific wonder, but of urgent need. The scientific demand that men should wait "till doomsday, or till such time as our senses and intellect working together may have raked in evidence enough" for answers to these questions, is, says James, "the queerest idol ever manufactured in the philosophic cave." We cannot wait for a final solution. Our daily life is full of choices that we cannot dodge, and some guide we simply must have. There can be no loitering at the crossroads. We are busy. We must choose, whether we will it or not, and where all is doubt, who shall refuse us the right to believe what seems most adapted to our needs? Not know, you understand, but believe.

That is the famous position taken in "The Will to Believe." As James has since pointed out, its real title should have been "The Right to Believe." No doctrine in James's thinking has been more persistently misunderstood. Yet it rests on the simplest of insights: that atheism and theism are both dogmas, for there is scientific evidence for neither; that to withhold judgment is really to make a judgment, and act as if God didn't exist; that until the evidence is complete men have a right to believe what they most need.

James has acted upon that right. He has made a picture compounded of the insights of feeling, the elaborations of reason, and the daily requirements of men. It is a huge guess, if you like, to be verified only at the end of the world. But it has made many men at home in the universe. And this democrat understood the need of feeling at home in the world, and he understood also that the aristocrats are not at home here. (Perhaps that's why they are aristocrats.) "The luxurious classes," he says, "are blind to man's real relation to the globe he lives on, and to the permanently hard and solid foundations of his higher life." And he prescribed for them—for their culture, I mean—this treatment: "To coal and iron mines, to freight trains, to fishing fleets in December, to dishwashing, clotheswashing and windowwashing, to road-building, and tunnel-making, to foundries and stokeholes, and to the frames of skyscrapers, would our gilded youths be drafted off according to their choice, to get the childishness knocked out of them, and to come back into society with healthier sympathies, and soberer ideas."

This, and thoughts like this, and kindnesses like this, put James not alone among the democrats of this uncertain world, but among the poets also; among the poetic philosophers who, like Goethe, Schopenhauer, and Whitman, have a sense of the pace of things. Sunlight and stormcloud, the subdued busyness of outdoors, the rumble of cities, the mud of life's beginning and the heaven of its hopes, stain his pages with the glad, sweaty sense of life itself.

It is an encouraging thought that America should have produced perhaps the most tolerant man of our generation. It is a stimulating thought that he was a man whose tolerance never meant the kind of timidity which refuses to take a stand "because there is so much to be said on both sides." As every one knows, he fought hard for his ideas, because he believed in them, and because he wanted others to believe in them. The propagandist was strong in William James. He wished to give as well as receive. And he listened for truth from anybody, and from anywhere, and in any form. He listened for it from Emma Goldman, the pope, or a sophomore; preached from a pulpit, a throne, or a soap-box; in the language of science, in slang, in fine rhetoric, or in the talk of a ward boss.

And he told his conclusions. He told them, too, without the expert's arrogance toward the man in the street, and without the dainty and finicky horror of being popular and journalistic. He would quote Mr. Dooley on God to make himself understood among men. He would have heard God gladly in the overalls of a carpenter, even though He came to preach that the soul of man is immortal. So open-minded was he; so very much of a democrat.

December, 1910

The experimental open-mindedness, the magnanimity and the vivid prose of William James, who died in 1910, the year Lippmann graduated from Harvard, had a lasting effect. Lippmann was twenty-one when he wrote this essay.

[*G.A.H.*]

Lincoln Steffens

I remember clearly the first time I ever saw Lincoln Steffens. He had been invited by the undergraduates of Harvard to speak to them at their regular Tuesday evening lecture in the Harvard Union. The hall was packed, and that means that there were some two thousand students present. I was one of them, and I think I know what brought us there. It was to hear some spicy stories about police graft and crooked politicians from the author of "The Shame of the Cities." We had not read the book, but we had heard about it, and the subject was exciting. Of Steffens we knew only that he was a muckraker. It was hard to imagine just what he would be like, but we were all men, and we could stand it. Those who were "up on things" pictured him to us as an angel with a flaming sword—a holy terror to sinners.

His smile surprised and puzzled us. We didn't understand it until the end of the speech. Steffens began with account of his work. He was a reporter, who had written about American government. Near the beginning he had found that mayors were the servants, not of their cities, but of political bosses—that Croker [Richard Croker, New York City boss around the turn of the century] and Ruef [Abe Ruef, a San Francisco labor boss] were more important than the man in the City Hall. But he had gone on. He had investigated the political boss, and had soon found that the boss, like the major, was only the tool of somebody else. The man higher up was the business boss,—Thomas F. Ryan was more important than Croker, Calhoun than Ruef. We were shocked. Dirty politics could be traced directly to bankers and presidents of street railways, to rich and powerful business men.

We promptly transferred our indignation from the hated political boss to the business boss. We were undergraduates, and we should gladly have hanged a few big business men. But Steffens didn't let us. He explained why these rich powerful men do what they do. He showed their temptation. He showed that they yielded to them because they had to do that, or give place to some one who didn't have scruples. He spoke of them without bitterness, with frank understanding, and he left us with the feeling that not men, but the conditions that make them, were the sources of wrong. "In my hunt through the cities, states and the nation," he said, "I have found that men are sound, willing to be good, eager to do right." That audience of college men cheered; there was a murmur of talk when it subsided, and for days I heard that sentence repeated in little groups arguing in a street corner, in the dining hall, at night in the dormitories.

For, you know, there is something convincing in the optimism of a man who has seen the worst. We thought we knew then why he could smile. But now that I have watched him at work, I think I understand it altogether. A political crook explained it. I imagined that a political crook would be the last man to feel kindly towards a muckraker. Yet one of them recently sent word by way of a mutual friend wishing Steffens a Merry Christmas. The friend asked the crook what interest he had in the man who roasts men like him. "Oh," said he, "he gives us hell, but he always lets us know before he gets through that he isn't any better than we are."

Steffens knows and believes that. His muckraking is done without a feeling of superiority. He does not pretend to be a better man than the people he exposes. He is not in the business of hauling bad people over the coals. He has muckraked himself, and has found pretty much the same kind of stuff that makes up crooks, bribe-takers, and tax dodgers. That's why he smiles with them.

December 28, 1910

When Lippmann was in his eighties, he remembered Lincoln Steffens as a "shocker," but he wrote this more flattering appraisal when he was twenty-one, flirting with reform, and grateful to Steffens with whom he was associated on Everybody's Magazine. *Steffens, looking for an assistant, had gone to Harvard to find "the best mind that could express itself in writing." He hired Lippmann who "caught on right away; keen, quiet, industrious, he understood the meaning of all that he learned." Steffens visited Russia in 1917 and 1919 and returned saying he had "seen the future and it works."*

[*G.A.H.*]

25

George Santayana

George Santayana's position at Harvard is peculiar. To thousands of students he is little more than a name to be mispronounced; to many, it must be confessed, he is the Mephistophelian intellect, the head and front of Denial, the reason that insidiously destroys faith. I am not exaggerating. I have talked to these men. Their fear is as genuine as that of Englishmen before Bradlaugh, of many Americans before [Robert] Ingersoll. The fact that they know Santayana by hearsay only increases their apprehension. Finally there is a very small group of men—perhaps ten in a class of four hundred—to whom Santayana is a cult.

There is a physical fascination about him. For a time we used to spend hours trying to understand that fascination. It was elusive, and it defied the pat characterization which is the chief amusement of the modern young man. Finally I hit upon the idea that if Leonardo's Mona Lisa were furnished with a little pointed beard, you would have a perfect portrait of Santayana. Walter Pater's description helped the analogy—"the head upon which all 'the ends of the world come,' and the eyelids are a little weary"; and again, "all the thoughts and experience of the world have etched and moulded there. . . ." So it seemed at least. One fellow nearly failed in one of his courses, because he found himself looking at Santayana instead of taking notes of what Santayana was saying. During a course on Plato, a friend of mine produced a caricature of Santayana arriving in Heaven to congratulate the angels upon their perfection. Another friend swore that the only adequate picture of Santayana was that of a kitten lying on its back teasing a world balanced upon its front paws.

Whether or not America can claim Santayana I don't know. He was born in Spain, but he came to America when he was very young, went to a public school in Boston, to college at Harvard, and with the exception of his summers which he spends at Oxford or in Spain, he has lived in Boston or Cambridge and has been a teacher at Harvard all his life. He has done his work in America. Yet he is as rare and as much an object of wonder in our civilization as an Italian missal on a news stand in the subway.

William James was part of us: he belonged spiritually to a generation which knew personally the pioneers who broke ground for civilization in the West. Santayana is in no sense a pioneer. He inherits a past. He belongs to the classical tradition of Europe—to an old, rich and complex civilization. William James was a symptom of that protestant mysticism which everywhere in America oozes through the commercialist exterior into Christian Science, New Thought, Shakerism or the Holy Jumpers. In James the "get there" quality of the man in the street, the belief in the great individual, stood with the unorganized democracy of Whitman. He is unthinkable anywhere else along the line of history. He would be as out of place as Oscar Wilde in Sparta. But Santayana might fit in almost any time after Plato. "I see by my little Spanish paper," said Santayana about two years ago, "that President Taft isn't very popular." And that is a good measure of his intimacy with contemporary American life.

As the Shavians and Ibsenites use the word, Santayana isn't a "modern." I believe it to be literally true that he isn't one because he is a thoroughly educated man. If he didn't know the history of thought as intimately as he does, he too might be running about as the discoverer of fresh eternal verities. . . .

The only excuse for the naïveté of the "moderns" is that they are good journalists. To be a good journalist is to understand how to insert an idea into the average man's head. Journalism consists in stating your idea so that somebody will believe it. It is not satisfied with possessing the truth. It insists that the truth shall come home to people. It is the glory of the "moderns" that they have discovered the uses of journalism, and it is no aspersion on their glory to say that a thoroughly educated man like Santayana is not aroused and startled by the originality of their ideas. It is simply intellectual candor. For as he once said: "The worst way to damn a man is to praise him for a virtue he doesn't possess."

But that applies equally to Santayana. The virtue he doesn't possess is the ability to speak to the men of his time. He has not bent himself to their habits of thought and to their language. He

27

has been satisfied to state his thought and to leave it. There is a cold perfection, a kind of vacant brilliancy about his style which was characterized by Max Beerbohm when he said that Walter Pater wrote English as if it were a dead language. You feel that Santayana has made a wonderful monument only to leave it standing in the attic. If he had the virtue of Bernard Shaw he would set it up in the middle of Times Square.

For that reason we are in danger of missing him. I find, for example, that lovers of poetry are not well acquainted with his verse. Yet anyone who pretends to a knowledge of contemporary poetry and ignores Santayana's little volume has seen "Hamlet" with Hamlet left out. His prose works, "The Life of Reason" particularly, are of course known to professional philosophers the world over. Several universities actually devote a course to him. His book on "Poetry and Religion" and the one on the philosophical poets —Lucretius, Dante and Goethe—are placed by an all too exclusive set of people among the greatest pieces of criticism ever written. The essay on Browning has been attacked by Chesterton and has made Santayana anathema in certain Boston literary quarters. The thing has a terrible finality about it.

Now it is almost impossible to-day to describe a philosophy like Santayana's with any assurance that the reader will recognize the meaning intended in the language. If I say that Santayana is a moralist, the first impulse is to think of your maiden aunt saying "thou shalt not." The word "morality" is in disgrace among spirited people because it has come in general usage to mean nothing but a few condemnations of cigarette-smoking, drinking, gambling and sexual license—a mere taboo upon personal vices. Your man or woman with an appetite for life is through with "morality" if it means simply "duty" or "right" or "loyalty" or some other sanctimonious abstraction. . . . As Santayana says, our current statements of morality have their basis "in authority rather than in human nature, and their goal in salvation rather than in happiness." In other words, the good people tell us to do what someone else thinks we ought to do instead of what we are fitted to do, because they want to "save" the world instead of making it happy.

Santayana is a moralist as the Greeks understood the word. "It seldom occurs to modern moralists," he says, "that theirs is the science of all good and the art of its attainment; they think only of some set of categorical precepts or some theory of moral sentiments abstracting altogether from the ideals reigning in society, in science, in art. They deal with the secondary question, What ought I to do? without having answered the primary question, What ought to be? They attach morals to religion rather than to politics, and this religion unhappily long ago ceased to be wisdom expressed in fancy in order to become superstition overlaid with reasoning. They divide man into compartments and the less they leave in the one labelled 'morality' the more sublime they think their morality is; and sometimes pedantry and scholasticism are carried so far that nothing but an abstract sense of duty remains in the broad region which should contain all human goods." Morality in this sense means an appraisal of all thought and all action in terms of human happiness. "The Life of Reason," Santayana's chief work, is an attempt at the beginning of the twentieth century to take stock of all the efforts men have made to make life happier. It's a brave effort to measure the contributions of the sciences, religions, arts, and political systems.

Of course, this is an appalling task. All that one man could pretend to do is to draw the outlines. I think Santayana has done so. I believe that the five volumes of "The Life of Reason" constitute the most nearly complete series of moral judgments made in modern times. And I say that with a full consciousness of its audacity. I say it remembering that Hegel and Emerson, Carlyle, Ibsen, Tolstoi, Nietzsche, Bernard Shaw and William James have all had their say in modern times. I do not deny that each of them has gone deeper into the lives of men than Santayana ever has or perhaps ever will. There is peril in trying to be complete. There is tremendous virtue in partial truths.

The serenity and aloofness of a Santayana shut him out of the rank of prophets. You feel at times that his ability to see the world steadily and whole is a kind of tragic barrier between him and the common hopes of ordinary men. It's as if he saw all forest and no trees. He filled active souls with a sense of the unbridgeable chasm between any ideal of perfection and the squeaky, rickety progress of human affairs. There is something of the pathetic loneliness of the spectator about him. You wish he would jump on the stage and take part in the show. Then you realize that he wouldn't be the author of "The Life of Reason" if he did. For it is a fact that a man can't see the play and be in it too.

It is extravagant to demand it. There should be nothing but gladness that this life of ours should have produced anything so nearly perfect. For however depressing the contrast between the stars and the mud puddle, there is a new dignity in mud puddles when they reflect the stars.

August, 1911

One of the philosophers, and also a graceful essayist, poet and novelist, who taught at Harvard when Lippmann was an undergraduate, George Santayana, like his student, came to wish for a "natural" aristocratic order that might guard mankind from the more debasing tendencies of popular sovereignty.

[*G.A.H.*]

Upton Sinclair

Mr. Upton Sinclair's intentions are so good; his sincerity so passionate; his earnestness so grim, and his self-analysis so humorless, that if you don't like his work, you feel as if you ought to keep quiet and wait for a verdict from posterity. For Mr. Sinclair's autobiographical writings are full of the deep conviction that he is a kind of Shelley—abused, maltreated, misunderstood as all poets and seers have been in their day. Every critical thrust is a repetition to him of the age-long persecution of genius; every inattentive ear is another sign of the world's stupidity. Fortified behind the tradition that to be great is to be misunderstood, Mr. Sinclair curses critics, publishers and public for not understanding him. So great is his belief that he is a poet haunted by a philistine world, that he has actually written a book which pretends to be the diary of a poet driven to suicide—"The Journal of Arthur Stirling" is nothing more nor less than Mr. Sinclair indulging in his favorite role, that of the young luminous Shelley, driven by poverty and humiliation to suicide.

If you look into your childhood, you will remember this mood which Upton Sinclair has never outgrown. You will remember being punished unjustly by a cruel and uncomprehending family. You will remember that while you sobbed on your bed, you had a picture of yourself dead—driven to death—by the cruelty of your family. You rather gloated over their regrets. And you felt hallowed and glorious and spiritual, like some chromo of the dead Chatterton. You enjoyed it a bit too, although you were terribly sincere. That mood has persisted down to this day in the writings of Upton Sinclair. It sits upon them like an incubus. His self-pity amounts almost to a disease, distorting his sense of life, pandering to a fussy, trivial egotism, obliterating all humor, exalting the prig, and turning his artistic production into a monotonous whine.

31

Worst of all, it has almost choked off the talent he possesses. For he can write eloquent description. In his civil war novel, "Manassas," there are battle scenes which are sharp and thrilling. He can make bullets whistle, horses charge and blood run with tremendous excitement. I don't know whether battles are fought in such an intense key. But granting that they are, Mr. Sinclair's battles are exciting and terrible and not easily forgotten.

The rest of this novel is an interesting narrative of the events from the Mexican War to John Brown's Raid. It is never dull. The novel ought, I think, to be called a successful retelling of history in story form. But even here Mr. Sinclair's uncorrected intensity prevents him from doing a great picture of that period. He seems never to have imagined that in those stirring times, there were people who weren't much stirred. His people do not live lives —they have intense feelings about slavery, and there is no hint that they ever have feelings about anything less exalted. Compare the book with Arnold Bennett's description of the siege of Paris in the "Old Wives Tale," and you will see the difference between sincere enthusiasm and a creative imagination. . . .

But that Mr. Sinclair has talent is proved by "The Jungle." It is the book that made him known. All his power of effective exaggeration is concentrated there. There is no need for me to tell over again the service that the book did. In a smaller way, it achieved a success similar to that of "Uncle Tom's Cabin." It affected politics, it changed public opinion; it was a blow at modern capitalism which shook its self-assurance. For that, Upton Sinclair deserves the thanks of all men. I, for one, should hate to pass on to a criticism of the bulk of his work without making it plain that "The Jungle" is as good a piece of agitation as the modern reform movement has produced. The test of its goodness is the fact that it made a nation listen. And if, as Mr. Sinclair himself is supposed to have said, the book, while intended to hit the American people in the head, really hit them in the stomach, the fault is not with the book. It didn't teach socialism as it was intended to; it did teach something about capitalism. That's a great deal. For socialism is too complex an idea to be accepted immediately. It requires an insight into capitalism. Mr. Sinclair has helped to furnish that.

When he tried to repeat this success by raking "society" fore and aft he failed. In "The Jungle" he had a theme suited to his talent. As in the battle scenes of "Manassas," the power to drive home brutal facts—raw, bloody, screaming facts—made "The Jungle" great. But when in "The Metropolis" he came to expose the vices of the rich, he had to deal with subtler, quiet things—with manners, with snobbishness, idleness of soul, with evils that are often attractive. He hated them as intensely as he had hated poisoned meat. He hated them so intensely that he hardly saw them. "High Society" couldn't see the reality, because of the wildness of Mr. Sinclair's emotions about it, and the world went on unimpressed.

"The Jungle," "The Metropolis," and "The Money Changers" are the products of his hate. It is a hate that is often splendid, that rarely understands. For Upton Sinclair is forever the dupe of his own sincerity, imagining that the intensity of his feeling is a substitute for a clear-eyed vision of fact.

Yet just such a vision a novelist must have who pretends to write about life to-day. This fresh sense of fact may not be all the artist requires, but it is surely something he must have: without it, the novelist wanders helplessly in that cloudy, hackneyed set of conventions which the average man calls a world. It is the business of all the great novelists to dispel those clouds, to substitute the true values of emotions for conventional ones, to separate, if you like, the big abstractions like Love, Beauty, Goodness to which the layman clings, into concrete passions and actual sensations.

That is why, perhaps, great novels have to win acceptance slowly. It is no easy thing for mankind, busy with its affairs, to give up its shortcuts and its easy generalizations for the puzzling variety of a real world. . . .

In "Love's Pilgrimage" Mr. Sinclair is playing Shelley again. It is the story of his genius against a world, wrong in business, wrong in sex, wrong in art, wrong from top to bottom. But it is all this wrong seen through the temperament of Mr. Sinclair's favorite alias. It is an attempt to give his mood, his suffering, his inspiration, his will power,—in short to handle things which cannot be handled with a club. . . .

The result is a book, which, for all its radical theory, is conventional and hackneyed to the point of exhaustion. He is always in an "agony of distress" or "transported with gratitude." He sits down "to receive the visits of his muse" and he goes in for "soul

terrifying toil." On two pages, we have "voicing utter desperation"
—"a brand upon my soul"—"racked his brains"—"after duly pon-
dering which communication"—and "cruel plight." Men don't
write that sort of stuff unless they think in those terms—and they
don't think in those terms if they see life directly.

Mr. Sinclair doesn't. What he sees is that haunting melodrama
about Shelley, and his book is a repetition of all the stale things
that have been said about abused genius. "He would spread his
wings to the glory of his vision; he would feel again the surge and
sweep of it, he would sing aloud with the power of it, and pledge
himself anew to live for it—if need be even to die for it. The world
was trying to crush it in him; the world hated it and feared it, and
was bound that it should not live; and Thyrsis had sworn to save
it—and so the issue was joined." You feel like advising Mr. Sinclair to stop writing about his Genius, and to try instead to write
about himself. For, if ever he could forget his own soul for a while,
he might come to gain the world through understanding it. . . .

It is a fairly general belief among critics, here and abroad, that
our literature is written by spinsters for school-girls. Often amusing
sometimes charming, American writing shirks life. It is lazy and
timid. Instead of taking up the high and difficult task of penetrating
human beings, and so revealing them, it has been content with the
ready-made and eminently proper, the easy generalization, and
the accepted sentimentality. The characters of contemporary American fiction are stockworn; they come not from original observa-
tion, but from the conventions of writing. They exist not from their
own inner vitality, but from a tradition about novels. And they
look upon a world incredibly bland and preposterously untrue.
They are agitated about problems which never agitate anybody. If
ever they are interested in the things that really interest human
beings, they behave as neither their author nor their readers could
possibly behave. You cannot send a man to American literature so
that he may enrich his experience and deepen his understanding.
You can merely pray that when he is confronted with the issues of
his life, he will forget completely what he has read. . . .

Here at least was a man dissatisfied with the existing order of
things. And so here, we might have expected a maturer insight. I,
at least, have not been able to find it. I have found effectiveness in
handling certain subjects, and a radicalism in thought. That isn't
enough. For radicalism can be as naive as a pink novel—yes, rad-

icalism can be entirely hackneyed. Mr. Sinclair's is, I think. For it springs from self-delusion, and is nourished on a convention.

December, 1911

Lippmann probably would have been just as unsympathetic to Upton Sinclair had he written about him fifty-seven years later, when Sinclair died. Lippmann saw no point in always *losing in politics, and Sinclair had been defeated five times as socialist candidate. Only in the Democratic race for governor of California in 1934, pledging to end poverty in California, did Sinclair come close to winning. He was a vegetarian, a teetotaler, and rather doctrinaire; Lippmann was none of these. Sinclair wrote many novels, all notable for moral earnestness, which did not, in Lippmann's opinion, compensate for their lack of creative imagination.*

[*G.A.H.*]

Lewis Jerome Johnson

Civil engineer and civic engineer, builder of the Harvard Stadium, leader in the Single Tax movement, author of an ideal charter for the city of Cambridge, propagandist for everything he believes in: Prof. Lewis Jerome Johnson of Harvard University is a tornado of efficient enthusiasm sweeping out the cobwebs of petty doubts, and the whole litter and rubbish of habits, caste-feeling, prejudice and snobbishness.

His pupils seem middle-aged and settled by comparison. He makes most people feel as if they were about half alive. Come within radiating distance of him, and if you have time to think of yourself, you'll feel like a listless, anemic putterer. In a few minutes you'll hear him go at a vested stupidity and smash it with a bludgeon of genial indignation which makes you want to laugh for joy at the sport of it. On top of indignation comes enthusiasm over a piece of democratic good news from Vancouver or Denmark, explained and expounded in spite of dinner, other engagements, and the routine of things. "Oh," he sighed to me once, "I can't stand it. Life's getting too interesting for me."

He hails you from across the street as you go sauntering along worrying about yourself. "You know," he will say, "the Grand Junction scheme for the recall is better than the Los Angeles one. Look here," and he fishes out of his green students' bag, charts, statistics, newspaper reports, and proves it to you then and there in the sunshine with the cars clanging by.

But his energy doesn't sputter. It has the quality of completing effectively whatever it undertakes. In the city of Cambridge they need among other things a new charter, for the present one is obviously a treasure for the Historical Society which preserves so carefully the Washington Elm and the minds of some of the inhabitants. So with a few others, principally engineers like himself, he set to work to draw up for Cambridge the most democratically efficient charter it was possible to devise. He went for his inspiration and for his models to the experiments of democrats the world over—to New Zealand, and Switzerland, to Des Moines, to U'Ren's work in Oregon. He studied their failures and their successes, and he helped write a charter based on their experience.

"But," protested a Boston banker, "it's all very well in New Zealand and Switzerland, but that doesn't prove it'll work in Massachusetts."

"Well, it works in Oregon, doesn't it?"

"Ah yes," replied the practical man to the theorist, "but Oregon isn't Massachusetts."

"I tell you," said Johnson, "what kind of proof you want. You want me to prove that it has worked well in Massachusetts for a hundred years. Then you'll be convinced that it'll work well in Massachusetts. You're not from Missouri: you're from Massachusetts."

He told about this encounter at a dinner of more or less radical college students. "It's high time," he continued, "that the applied scientist took a hand in politics. We engineers are taught to make things for people to use and enjoy. We build bridges for men, not for dividends. When government is handled as an applied science, our politics will be as good as our bridges."

Men are bothered at first by all the precision and accuracy and efficiency of minds like his. They wonder, as I did, whether it means not only the end of waste and confusion but of beauty too, and the sense of wonder.

On the night of President Lowell's inauguration we marched to the Stadium by classes, carrying torches. There was a good deal of parading, and cheering, and speech-making. I met Professor Johnson the next day, and I asked him what he thought of our performance.

"Well, to tell you the truth, I didn't see much of it. I was watching the Stadium." It was the first time I had heard him comment about the thing he had built. "I was looking at the sweep of it. It was fine by the October light." I was satisfied, assured that the precision and accuracy of the scientist is coming not only to end waste, but to create things of use, and to enjoy them in their highest use, which is beauty.

February, 1912

37

Paul Mariett

October 24, 1888—March 14, 1912

In the Spring of 1910, six of us, with one exception undergraduates in Harvard College, used to eat dinner together about as often as we could induce an unwilling secretary to send out postcards and collect the group. We had begun with no small amount of self-consciousness by regarding each other as types; a claim to membership was as poet, dramatist, musician, scientist, romantic, reformer. After dinner we would gather about a fire and start a discussion. Inevitably the topic of the evening seemed to involve all human interests, so that arguments about religion would end in a quarrel over Chesterton's sanity and considerable heartsearching as to whether soap and socialism were really middle-class fads. Those evenings are memorable in many ways, but chiefly for what they gave us of Paul Mariett.

Not long after, the tumor of which he died took hold of him. That Spring he overflowed with life: feeling his own power, he was full of plans, and the grim silence which he had formerly maintained began to break into colorful confidence. His appetite, for everything, was enormous. Almost for the first time we began to see that the real Paul was a fellow of turbulent interests and subtle perceptions, who had carefully protected himself by a brusque and unsociable manner. Beneath the austerity was a brilliant, vivid, and audacious love of living. He was shy about his delicacies and bashful about his virtues; his vices he loved to parade. Paul rather enjoyed the reputation of being something of a man-eater. Of all things he did not want, the prettifying touch is, I believe, the one he despised most. He himself was brutally direct; he liked others to be so, too. For all the conventional attitudinizing of the poet over sweetness and light he had a bitter scorn; he could hate with zest; he believed that hate was a good robust virtue. To

38

all kinds of softness Paul was a hard bed indeed, and to muffled personalities and finicky souls he was a cleansing gale.

You had to brace your feet to meet him—there was no chance to shirk behind a graceful pose, or a cultivated one, or any other kind of barrier between yourself and him. That was his genius: people became closer knit and more self-contained when he was around. You could not coddle your difficulties in him, for he made you ashamed of your slackness.

Paul enjoyed life. He had, it seemed, no listless pleasures. When he ate it was with tremendous relish; a book was something to be attacked and beaten till he had subordinated it; swimming and snowshoeing he loved partly for the strain and rack of them. He had us all intimidated by his interest in boxing. Languages Paul seemed to learn with no trouble at all. For a time he carried a Portuguese translation of the Gospels in his pocket in order to teach himself Portuguese. The classics he knew,—they were a natural background to a really vast culture which he absorbed silently. With his music, and his languages and literatures, he was a peculiarly learned undergraduate. Yet he hated pedantry so vigorously, and showed so terse and unacademic a manner, that not even his closest friends were entirely aware of the very solid foundations of Paul's literary interests.

This learning did not dull his appetite for existence, and that is what distinguishes him from most undergraduate poets. They like life nicely selected, and their passions are carefully strained through a literary tradition. No doubt they often sing melodiously and show surprising competence in verse. But their passions are Swinburne's or Shelley's; somebody else has sweated for them. Paul Mariett was too genuine a lover of life to accept some one else's version of it. He struggled violently, sometimes aimlessly, against the ordinary technique of passion, like a man caught in a snarl of rope. Now and again he would half free himself: I think some of the poems in this volume prove that. But the struggle was only at its beginning when he was felled by the disease which finally killed him. It is our faith that with time he would have won.

The tragic feeling which runs through so much of his work is, I am sure, not entirely ordinary undergraduate pessimism. It is a genuinely tragic feeling, a gift of nature's rather than a handicap. Nietzsche speaks of the pessimism of strength and describes it as "an intellectual predilection for what is hard, awful, evil, problematical in existence, owing to well-being, to exuberant health, to *fullness* of existence." In Paul Mariett, the tragic is always active, sharp and colored; it was not so much a regret over life as an insight into it. . . .

His illness lasted two years. After a while no opiate dulled the agony he suffered night and day. It was an inexplicable affliction, —one of those terrors in existence for which philosophies and religions have not yet accounted. Paul Mariett had only his sheer human valor to oppose to it. He stood his fate; racked in body, his soul was never sick.

1913

Written as a preface to The Poems of Paul Mariett, *this is the only sketch Lippmann published of someone who was not a prominent public personality.*

[*G.A.H.*]

John Reed

Though he is only in his middle twenties and but five years out of Harvard, there is a legend of John Reed. It began, as I remember, when he proved himself to be the most inspired song and cheer leader that the football crowd had had for many days. At first there was nothing to recommend him but his cheek. That was supreme. He would stand up alone before a few thousand undergraduates and demonstrate without a quiver of self-consciousness just how a cheer should be given. If he didn't like the way his instructions were followed he cursed at the crowd, he bullied it, sneered at it. But he always captured it. It was a sensational triumph, for Jack Reed wasn't altogether good form at college. He came from Oregon, showed his feelings in public, and said what he thought to the club men who didn't like to hear it.

Even as an undergraduate he betrayed what many people believe to be the central passion of his life, an inordinate desire to be arrested. He spent a brief vacation in Europe and experimented with the jails of England, France, and Spain. In one Spanish village he was locked up on general principles, because the King happened to be passing through town that day. The next incident took place during the Paterson strike. Reed was in town less than twenty-four hours before the police had him in custody. He capped his arrest by staging the Paterson strike pageant in Madison Square Garden, and then left for Europe to live in a Florentine villa, where he was said to be hobnobbing with the illegitimate son of Oscar Wilde, and to be catching glimpses of Gordon Craig. He made speeches to Italian syndicalists and appointed himself to carry the greetings of the American labor movement to their foreign comrades. He bathed in a fountain designed by Michelangelo and became violently ill. He tried high romance in Provence. One night, so he says, he wrestled with a ghost in a haunted house, and was thrown out of bed.

He lived in those days by editing and writing for *The American Magazine*. But that allegiance couldn't last. Reed wasn't meant for sedate family life, and he broke away to join the staff of the *Masses*. They advertised him as their jail editor, but as a matter of fact he was the managing editor, which even on the *Masses* carries with it a prosaic routine. For a few weeks Reed tried to take the *Masses'* view of life. He assumed that all capitalists were fat, bald, and unctuous, that reformers were cowardly or scheming, that all newspapers are corrupt, that [socialist leader] Victor Berger and the Socialist party and Samuel Gompers and the trade unions are a fraud on labor. He made an effort to believe that the working class is not composed of miners, plumbers, and workingmen generally, but is a fine statuesque giant who stands on a high hill facing the sun. He wrote stories about the night court and plays about ladies in kimonos. He talked with intelligent tolerance about dynamite, and thought he saw an intimate connection between the cubists and the I.W.W. He even read a few pages of Bergson.

But it was only a flirtation. Reed's real chance came when the *Metropolitan Magazine* sent him to Mexico. All his second-rate theory and propaganda seemed to fall away, and the public discovered that whatever John Reed could touch or see or smell he could convey. The variety of his impressions, the resources and color of his language seemed inexhaustible. The articles which he sent back from the border were as hot as the Mexican desert, and Villa's revolution, till then reported only as a nuisance, began to unfold itself into throngs of moving people in a gorgeous panorama of earth and sky. Reed loved the Mexicans he met, loved them as they were, marched with them, raided with them, danced with them, drank with them, risked his life with them. He had none of the condescension of the foreigner, no white man's superiority. He was not too dainty, or too wise, or too lazy. Mexicans were real people to him with whom he liked to be. He shared their hatred of the *cientificos,* he felt as they did about the church, and he wrote back to us that if the United States intervened to stop the revolution he would fight on Villa's side.

He did not judge, he identified himself with the struggle, and gradually what he saw mingled with what he hoped. Wherever his sympathies marched with the facts, Reed was superb. His interview with Carranza [leader of the Constitutional Party, which took power in Mexico in August, 1914] almost a year ago was so sensationally accurate in its estimate of the feeling between Carranza and Villa that he suppressed it at the time out of loyalty to the success of the revolution. But where his feeling conflicted with the facts, his vision flickered. He seems totally to have misjudged the power of Villa.

Reed has no detachment, and is proud of it, I think. By temperament he is not a professional writer or reporter. He is a person who enjoys himself. Revolution, literature, poetry, they are only things which hold him at times, incidents merely of his living. Now and then he finds adventure by imagining it, oftener he transforms his own experience. He is one of those people who treat as serious possibilities such stock fantasies as shipping before the mast, rescuing women, hunting lions, or trying to fly around the world in an aeroplane. He is the only fellow I know who gets himself pursued by men with revolvers, who is always once more just about to ruin himself.

I can't think of a form of disaster which John Reed hasn't tried and enjoyed. He has half-spilled himself into commercialism, had his head turned by flattery, tried to act like a cynical war correspondent, posed as a figure out of Ibsen. But always thus far the laughter in him has turned the scale, his sheer exuberance has carried him to better loves. He is many men at once, and those who have tried to bank on some phase of him, to regard him as a writer, a correspondent, a poet, a revolutionist, or a lover, lose him. There is no line between the play of his fancy and his responsibility to fact; he is for the time the person he imagines himself to be.

Reed is one of the intractables, to whom the organized monotony and virtue of our civilization are unbearable. You would have to destroy him to make him fit. At times when he seemed to be rushing himself and others into trouble, when his ideas were especially befuddled, I have tried to argue with him. But all laborious elucidation he greets with pained boredom. He knows how to dismiss in a splendid flourish the creature

> Who wants to make the human race and me
> March to a geometric Q. E. D.

I don't know what to do about him. In common with a whole regiment of his friends I have been brooding over his soul for years, and often I feel like saying to him what one of them said when Reed was explaining Utopia, "If I were establishing it, I'd hang you first, my dear Jack." But it would be a lonely Utopia.

December 26, 1914

John Reed, unlike his Harvard classmate Lippmann, was an enthusiastic witness of the Russian revolution, which he described in Ten Days That Shook the World, *for which Lenin wrote a foreword. Reed was twice indicted for sedition, died of typhus at thirty-three, and was buried in the Kremlin.*

[G.A.H.]

Sigmund Freud

In discussions of Freud's work, the perfect bromide is to say that his theories are exaggerated. They may be, for all we know. Since the history of scientific thought makes it clear that later research modifies practically every hypothesis, it is altogether safe to insist that Freud's theories will appear crude to men of the future. Yet in the mouths of laymen, and even of ordinary neurologists, the remark is a most uninteresting truth. When made by people who have neither the knowledge nor the technique to understand or to criticize Freud, the comment is sheer platitude. They do not know wherein he exaggerates; they cannot give evidence that he does. They simply take a chance and assert it. It is as if I walked into the Rockefeller Institute, spent an hour or two in Dr. Noguchi's [Hideyo Noguchi, renowned medical researcher on yellow fever] laboratory, shook my head gravely, and remarked: "Well, you'll see. Much of what you are doing will be thrown aside by your successors." Wouldn't Dr. Noguchi reply with great politeness, "No doubt you are right, but how do you know you are right?" And wouldn't I be entitled to feel that I had made a remark about as helpful as that of the small boy who stands by the roadside and advises passing motorists to get a horse?

Yet people will criticize Freud on the basis of a dinner-table conversation or perhaps on the reading of his book about *The Interpretation of Dreams*. I have heard physicians deny the theory that dreams are realized wishes, on the ground that people are subject to nightmares. They seem to think that in the lifetime which Freud has devoted to the study of dreams he might possibly have overlooked the nightmares. I have heard laymen resist the theory of infantile sexuality, because in their opinion children have no sexuality. Yet they would not dare for a moment to raise such offhand objections to the latest discovery in physics and chemistry;

45

they would assume that a man who has become the center of world-wide scientific discussion would have taken account of at least the obvious objections to his theories.

It is clear why we who are laymen cannot remain entirely passive about Freud, why we cannot sit still and listen and simply try to understand. We ourselves are the subject matter of his science, and in a most intimate and drastic way. The structure of matter can be left to objective analysis, but these researches of Freud challenge the very essence of what we call ourselves. They involve the sources of our character, they carry analysis deeper into the soul of man than analysis has ever been carried before. The analysis hurts, but even superficially there is enough compelling truthfulness about it to make an easy escape impossible. We recognize in the analysis items that we have never quite dared phrase even to ourselves, and it is not possible to repel the attack altogether. Freud has a way of revealing corners of the soul which we believed were safe from anybody's knowledge. This uncanny wisdom is to most people both fascinating and horrible. They can neither take hold nor let go. So they rationalize their difficulty and build out of it a defensive compromise. They say that Freud is a clever man but that he exaggerates, that there is some truth in his teaching and much untruth. There is no better way than this of holding an idea at arm's length. It enables us to escape its consequences by blunting its force.

The Freudians themselves are well aware that they cannot at present hope for a really disinterested discussion. If the arguments of archaeologists and chemists cannot be conducted without the injection of passionate prejudice, what hope is there for argument about passionate prejudice itself? Because Freud is discussing the very nature of interest it becomes very difficult to consider Freud disinterestedly. The defenses which we set up against a revelation of ourselves, he disintegrates at the outset. The challenge is so subtle and so radical that our whole organism seems to concentrate for resistance.

Our attitude is like that of a lady with whom I once went to a bull-fight. She thought the spectacle horrible, so she held her hand over her eyes. Then by looking between her fingers she watched the fight. Freud's theory has much the same attraction and repulsion. Our craving for it and our resistance to it are both below the level of reason, and our intellectual attitude is very largely determined by this conflict. And as civilized people try to conceal the fact that they are deeply disturbed, the fascination and the tendency to withdraw neutralize each other in the conscious mind, and the product is to the effect that Freud carries his ideas too far. The lady, when she spoke to her friends later about the bull-fight, said nothing about the fight. She said the Spanish costumes were very picturesque.

The difficulties of relating ourselves to a teaching like Freud's are, however, part of a larger problem. We live in a world where knowledge is becoming more and more highly specialized, and as laymen we cannot hope to have the equipment for really adequate judgment. The day is gone when we could turn for guidance to someone whose authority was unquestioned. Even science, which is the surest method of knowledge we have, is based on the denial of infallibility in any scientist. We assume that Darwin or Freud must be wrong on innumerable points. But we do not know enough to say when and where they are wrong. We are called upon to make decisions which we are not trained to make. This is almost the central problem of the modern intellectual life. How shall we distribute our faith without going it blind, how shall we have the loyalty to believe without losing the capacity to doubt? How much trust shall we put in a man like Freud, for example? How can we react in a way that will not stultify, either by petty resistance or petty acceptance?

We cannot begin to test his facts nor follow his experiments. But what we can do is to get the sense of his method and the quality of his mind. We can say that we recognize in him or fail to recognize in him the type of imagination, the sense of reality, the honesty before fact, the logical penetration, and the background of experience which are likely to yield fruitful results. We know in a general way the qualities of thought which lead to important conclusions. No doubt truths have been reached in other ways, by tossing a coin, or guessing, or saying vehemently whatever happens to be vegetating in the mind. But truths reached this way have to pass a much closer scrutiny than truths which are the normal products of what we call the scientific spirit. In the complexity of specialized knowledge our best guide is to test the working of the thinker's mind. For our first credulity it will probably serve more accurately than any other.

In such a test Freud would, I believe, emerge triumphant over practically all of his lay opponents, and most of his professional ones. There has rarely been a great theory worked out so close to actual practice, an hypothesis that has been so genuinely pragmatic in origin. Freud is first of all a physician, an applied scientist using his theory to carry him forward in dealing with his patients. The amount of industry that the psycho-analytic method requires is an added guarantee of his good faith. He has offered no short cut; in fact, one of the real objections raised by his critics is the time needed to make an analysis. He has formulated no immutable doctrine; the history of his career is the history of opinion bending and modifying before experience.

When I compare his work with the psychology that I studied in college, or with most of the material that is used to controvert him, I cannot help feeling that for his illumination, for his steadiness and brilliancy of mind, he may rank among the greatest who have contributed to thought. I know how easy it is to be deceived, but I take it that this is a small risk in comparison with the necessity for recognizing in his own lifetime a man of outstanding importance. After all, there were people who welcomed Darwin, and saw how profoundly he must affect our thinking. In Freud I believe we have a man of much the same quality, for the theories that have grown from his clinic in Vienna have always flowered in endless ways. From anthropology through education to social organization, from literary criticism to the studies of religions and philosophies, the effect of Freud is already felt. He has set up a reverberation in human thought and conduct of which few as yet dare to predict the consequences.

April 17, 1915

Lippmann's appreciation of Freud, written for The New Republic *in 1915, was one of the first articles in a nonprofessional American publication to call attention to the historical importance of the work of the Viennese psychoanalyst. A year earlier Lippmann had had a lengthy conversation about Freud with Leonard Woolf in England, and Woolf wrote of their talk: "There are few things more unexpected and more exciting than suddenly finding someone of intelligence and understanding who at once with complete frankness will go with one below what is the usual surface of conversation and discussion."*

[G.A.H.]

Warren G. Harding

If an optimist is a man who makes lemonade out of all the lemons that are handed to him, then Senator Harding is the greatest of all optimists. He has been told by his friends and his critics that he is colorless and without sap, commonplace and dull, weak and servile. Right you are, says the Senator. You have described exactly the kind of man this country needs. It has tried [Theodore] Roosevelt and Wilson, and look. It can't stand the gaff. I am nothing that they were. I am no superman like Roosevelt and no superthinker like Wilson. Therefore, I am just the man you are looking for. How do I know that? I am distinguished by the fact that nothing distinguishes me. I am marked for leadership because I have no marks upon me. I am just the man because no one can think of a single reason why I am the man. If any one happens to think of a reason then I shall cease to be that normal man which these abnormal times demand.

Just what is Mr. Harding trying to say anyway? Presumably some idea is lodged in his brain and panting for utterance beyond the normal human impulse to find a good reason for his own candidacy. For the sake of good appearances in history, I suppose that Mr. Harding is not exalting his defects as do the pretenaturally wise animals in Clarence Day's *This Simian World*. He can't just be the one-eyed man who is against two-eyed men, or the tortoise who thinks the hare leads too fast a life. Some other idea is sprouting on that front porch in Marion.

That idea, probably, is that the Presidency has grown too big for any man, and that the time has come for decentralizing its power. There are conceivably two ways this might be done. One way would be to think out a plan for adapting responsible cabinet government to the congressional system. It is a way that would require an abnormal lot of thinking. It would require also a quarrel

49

with Congress. For until Congress disgorges its petty control over the details of administration, Congress will not be fit to take upon itself major control of executive policy. But Congress at present is so much concerned with the things that do not belong to it, that it has no opportunity to be concerned with the things that do. The relation of Congress to administration is like that of a general staff so tremendously interested in the second lieutenants that it ignores the lieutenant-generals. The result is that the general can't command the lieutenants, and the lieutenants' hair is forever standing on end while they try to obey the swivel chairs. Mr. Harding's remedy for this is to sack the general and find someone who will be content with four stars and will keep his mouth shut.

There is something in it. If you can't think of any way to redistribute the functions of government, then all you have to do is to find a President who will be so weak that power will leave him. That is the inner meaning of Mr. Harding's nomination. He was put there by the Senators for the sole purpose of abdicating in their favor. The Grand Dukes have chosen their weak Tsar in order to increase the power of the Grand Dukes. And if he is elected the period will be known in our constitutional history as the Regency of the Senate.

What will this accomplish? It will reduce the prestige and the power of the White House. Will it create a better balance of prestige and power in the whole government? Hardly. The gentlemen who intend to benefit by Mr. Harding's abnormal normality are a group tiny enough to meet in a hotel bedroom. They are not the elected Congress of the United States. Their rise to power would mean not the restoration of a balance between executive and legislature but the substitution of government by a clique for the lonely majesty of the President. Dangerous as is the plight we are in, it has at least the advantage of visibility. The President may be an autocrat, yet every one knows where that autocrat lives. But the government of a clique, an invisible, self-invited collection of friends, would be just nothing but the return of exactly what every decent person has fought against for a generation.

That the glory of the normal should be presented to a weary nation as the purest Republican doctrine according to the Fathers is one of those paradoxes which Mr. Chesterton says, always sit beside the wells of truth. It is in fact primitive Democratic doctrine. That doctrine has always been that anybody could govern, that leadership was dangerous, excellence somewhat un-American, and specialized knowledge somewhat sinister. The Republicans from Hamilton's time on have always professed belief that ability mattered, and that no system of government could succeed in which the best men were not preeminent. They may have had some queer notions about what constituted the best men, but they have at least done this republic the service of refusing to accept the idea that anybody could do anything. They have not in theory at least stooped to encourage the democratic vices. Mr. Harding does. I hate to say it, but he is in ultimate theory a great deal closer to [William Jennings] Bryan than he is to any great Republican from Hamilton to Root. For Mr. Bryan has that same simple faith that any deserving fellow can do anything, which Mr. Harding has now brought forth from the caverns of his mind.

July 21, 1920

The 1920 Republican Presidential candidate was a front man for the "Ohio gang" and big business, whose administration would be beset by corruption and whose White House, as historian Samuel Eliot Morrison wrote, would have the atmosphere of a bar-room.

[G.A.H.]

James Cox

The election [1920] comes either too late or too soon, for it most certainly comes at a time when the voters at large are not sharply divided on anything that either party has to offer. Nine months ago there was a divided opinion about the treaty. There is still a divided opinion, but there is no very strong opinion except among a comparatively few. There are fierce irreconcilables and there are warm leaguers, but if the politicians who know their business are a gauge of what the public cares about, then the American voters today expect nothing from either party.

For what did the two parties do?

Did they select candidates who represented the issue on which the solemn referendum was to be taken? They did not. They avoided such candidates. They avoided [Hiram] Johnson and [Herbert] Hoover at Chicago, and anybody who was identified with Wilson, at San Francisco. The Republicans picked a man whose view on the League [of Nations] no human being could discern, and the Democrats picked a man who had never up to the time of his nomination identified himself nationally with the League in any memorable way. In fact, so irrelevant were both candidates to the issue that was supposed to divide them, that the newspapers actually waited breathlessly to find out whether Mr. Harding was for the Republican reservations and whether James Cox was orthodox.

And then to cap the climax, the Democratic chairman blurted out an interview one warm day in Washington saying that we weren't to become too much excited about the whole thing. He was, of course, promptly spanked and silenced, but a truth is not so easily expunged. Those who discount the words that politicians use and watch their acts find it hard to create the illusion for themselves that the issue between the two parties is isolation as against cooperation. As a campaign stunt it may be effective to show that the Republicans are committed to the policy of the armed hermit, because Hiram Johnson has blessed Warren G. Harding. But no one who knows American politics is deceived. For he knows that in the future as in the past, Johnson may count before election but Murray Crane [Republican Senator from Massachusetts] and the Easterners count *after* election. They know that campaign speeches *now* count for very little, later. They note that the Republican friends of the League are, on the whole, remaining Republican. And those who are not entangled in words feel morally certain that the extent and the character of American participation will be determined not before November, but after. It will be determined not by the vote of the people but by the logic of facts.

As they discount Mr. Harding's vague opposition, so do they discount Mr. Cox's induced emotion. Mr. Cox is a clever and shrewd politician in buoyant health. He is a good judge of what is expedient, and he is a facile journalist. He has the gift of discerning when there is a mass of votes not too much affected by principle or conviction. He is also an excellent judge of what constitutes the necessary minimum of principle in order to satisfy the small groups of people who care deeply about such things. He does not exceed that minimum. Yet he has such an air of vitality and certainty that, unless you look closely, you imagine that the exuberance of the salesmanship is the virtue of the goods.

No man, for example, could have said less for the League than Mr. Cox did in his acceptance speech, and remained a Democrat in good standing. The columns of newsprint which he devoted to the subject turn out, on analysis, to commit him only to some undefined form of ratification. From the point of view of what is actually going on in the world abroad, this position does not differ one iota from that of almost any Republican reservationist. For the moot questions of the League are not whether an ambassador shall sit at Geneva, but whether in a tangible sense America will guarantee the covenants of the League and the terms of the settlement. The real decision turns on concrete questions of diplomacy—on Poland, the German reparations, the Balkans, Asia Minor, the Pacific, Africa—on whether America will share responsibility because she has helped to decide actual policy, or whether she will attend the formal sessions, and miss the point of the real negotiations. There is nothing in Mr. Cox's speeches or in his experience

53

to indicate that under his guidance America will not be the wall-flower in the Council of the League. There is not even evidence that Mr. Cox knows how to dance.

There are a few Americans who were abroad and some who stayed at home who have actually learned something of what Europe is. Neither Mr. Harding nor Mr. Cox has. They are purely domestic. They have lived their lives in local politics, and they think as local politicians. The League they are talking about is that fragment of it which endangered the friendly relations between a Democratic President and a Republican Congress. The bulk of the League, which is in Europe, does not really enter into their consciousness, nor do the conditions which it confronts. There were candidates for whom the League was a vivid reality, but neither Mr. Cox nor Mr. Harding is such a candidate. Neither of them would of his own conviction have elected to make the League a supreme issue. Both of them are driven to it by influences that they cannot offend.

Broadly speaking what happened is that popular interest was suffocated by the later phases of the treaty debate. The bulk of the audience went home before the show was over. There remained behind, two groups of irreconcilables—the Johnson group and the Wilson group. Both were vehement, small in number, but of strategic importance. Johnson controls several necessary states; Wilson is the head of the federal organization. The party managers understood the situation, and in both conventions they followed exactly the same line. They gave the irreconcilables the platform, and took for themselves the control of the parties and the nomination of the candidates. The irreconcilables won a verbal victory, but the professional politicians secured the substance. The substance for them was not pro-League or anti-League. They were indifferent to the League, and they took it that the mass of the voters were also tolerably indifferent. They were content, even pleased, to have the debate rage about platforms, for it distracted attention from the important fact, which is: that in the Republican Party the old machine has conquered and obliterated the Bull Moose; that in the Democratic Party the local Tammanys have conquered and obliterated the highbrows, and the silk-stockings, and the mugwumps.

I said that the election came too late or too early. Had it come nine months ago when the hopeless deadlock began in Washington, it would have been an election between Wilson's internationalism and Henry Cabot Lodge's nationalism. Were it to come a year or so in the future the issues of American reconstruction might have crystallized.

Coming betwixt and between, when an old issue has faded and before new ones have been defined, it is inevitably an unreal choice. Its unreality is attested by the fact that neither candidate embodies the ideas for which nominally he stands. It is unreal because both candidates are the products of intra-party struggle for control, and the meaning of their candidacies lies in that control. Their speeches and platforms are concessions to minorities, and pure bewilderment to the majority. Under cover of that bewilderment the work of Theodore Roosevelt and Woodrow Wilson passes into history. Their spirit controls neither party today.

And one man's guess is as good as the other's about where and how the creative spirit in American life will next appear.

October, 1920

As far as Lippmann was concerned, the Presidential election of 1920 was fought between two nonentities—Harding—and his weaselly Democratic opponent, the governor of Ohio, James Cox. Cox was nominated on the forty-forth ballot and got nine million votes to Harding's 16 million.

[*G.A.H.*]

H. G. Wells

Two years ago, when the fighting in France came to an end, many people were at a loss. The war had a most paradoxical effect on them. For, while it was disarranging the universe at large, it was providing cultivated people with the most orderly spiritual universe they had ever lived in. Black was black, white was white, sheep were sheep and goats were goats. In all their lives the distinction between right and wrong, between glorious friend and unspeakable foe, had never been so absolutely clear. Men and women could love and hate without a sickly doubt. They felt completely at home in the world. If they were puzzled for a moment, the government soon reassured them. If they wished facts, the newspapers in no uncertain tone soon supplied them. It was a thoroughly reliable world while it lasted.

Unfortunately it disappeared the day after the armistice. What remained was a shattered world outside, and a buzzing blooming confusion within the minds of men. How were they to feel about the world now? Some of them said: let us pretend that the armistice is an illusion and that there is no victory; let us carry on the war as usual. The people who took this line counted heavily at the Peace Conference. Others said: let us pretend that the war never took place. Our boys fought gloriously and ought always to be remembered. Beyond that, the time has come to behave as if nothing had happened since the tragedy at Buffalo which made a President out of Vicepresident Roosevelt. The people who felt this way counted heavily at the Chicago convention. Others said: let us pretend that we have realized our vision; let us act as if a new world were born.

But there were still others who could not stomach Paris or Chicago or the White House and denied the pretensions of all three. They knew the war was over, but they knew also that the effects of the war would be felt through all their lives; and they were certain

56

that, while the vision of the war had not been realized, it was the vision to which they wanted somehow to dedicate themselves.

"Dedicate" is a large word, and "somehow" is a vague word, but they are appropriate to the mood of sensitive men and women almost anywhere. For in spite of appearances, a generous portion of mankind really meant what they said when they called this a war to end war, and insisted that such a catastrophe must never happen again. They meant it, in spite of politicians and orators who did not mean it, and they mean it now. The impulse is there; it lacks illumination and guidance, and neither is to be had and neither is to be expected from busy and worried politicians. The ordinary shibboleths will serve for a political campaign, but they are too feeble to enlist enthusiasm or to arouse opposition. And so the whole performance goes on because the law stipulates that it shall go on. But, for the most part, people regard it absent-mindedly. They are searching for an order of ideas that they do not find in editorials and the speeches of public men. Wherever there is a mind at work, there, also, is a feeling that the cocksure people are rather quaint and that they do not matter much. There has come an inevitable pause after the violence and the fatigue of an experience beyond the immediate comprehension. But it is an expectant pause.

While it lasts, the creative and the critical spirit are in abeyance. In their place, reign for a brief moment those impulses which the civilized man regards as his uncivilized inheritance. There prevails an epidemic of fear about everybody who does not think exactly like ourselves; enormous intolerance; a vast amount of strutting and issuing of defiances, and refusing to confer, and declining to compromise; an outburst of bad manners against all other nations; and, on the whole, an exhibition of senseless and unmanly jumpiness about lurking perils, most of them hallucinations and the rest of them quite certainly manageable, given a modicum of courage and common sense. There has been an eruption from below, because the better conscience is puzzled and preoccupied and distracted. That conscience does not work except where it has a convincing picture of the origin and destiny of man.

Even before the war it was doubtful whether the modern man had a convincing picture of the universe. In 1905, [G. K.] Chesterton was complaining in *Heretics* that "a man's opinion on tramcars matters; his opinion on Botticelli matters; his opinion on all things does not matter. He may turn over and explore a million objects, but he must not find that strange object, the universe; for if he does, he will have a religion, and be lost. Everything matters— except everything." This was by way of introduction to a book on such men as [George Bernard] Shaw and [H. G.] Wells.

To-day the case is different. Mr. Shaw has completed his bible of the life of man. Mr. Wells has written an Outline of History. The moderns have set out to find the universe. They have learned from the war that an opinion on all things matters supremely, and that men are stumped for lack of a universe. They can deal with nothing effectively until they recover a sense of their relationship to things at large, until they feel once more their position in space and their part in the marches of time. That is the kind of illumination the modern man needs, needs for his composure, needs in order to steady his attention, in order to focus his interest, to renew his courage, and revive his incentive. He cannot improvise an illumination of such scope. It must come to him as a free gift from genius, from some of those invaluable men who happen along occasionally with the ability to give hearing to the deaf and sight to the blind.

Mr. H. G. Wells is unmistakably such a man. His mind is an extension of the ordinary citizen's mind, an instrument, which like the telephone, the microscope and the telescope, gives a powerful supplement to our senses and our reason. In the company of Wells you are enlarged, vague feelings tend to become lucid, obscure aspiration becomes orderly, the tangled experience of life takes form. The issues which exercise Wells are not those of the specialist. He is not the greatest living expert on any one subject. But he is the greatest living consumer of the results arrived at by the expert. It is a synthetic genius, and that is a very rare and a very high form of genius. It consists in the ability to relate the results of research to practical conduct.

It is not popularization. Wells does not merely tell in a simple and attractive form what historians or biologists are teaching. He is if you like the man who makes the map out of a thousand partial surveys, or the architect who makes the design of a house out of the special craft of the steel maker, mason, plumber, and carpenter. He represents the last stage in the making of knowledge, the stage of the finished product adapted to human use. There are scores of men, for example, who know more expertly every phase of human history. There is no man in our world who can approach him in sheer capacity for bringing that knowledge to bear upon the complexities of the modern world.

It is a truism to say that there is no final account of human history. All historical writing is a selection by some standard. Often the standard is an unconscious bias in the historian, as when he is bent on glorifying his king; sometimes it is a deliberate bias, as when he writes history to justify his country's claim to a piece of territory; sometimes it is a critical bias, as when he sets out to deflate the pretensions of some ancient institution or an honoured figure; sometimes it is a specialist's bias, as when he sets out to show that a certain formula has governed human relations.

Mr. Wells has an avowed bias, a candid purpose in undertaking the enormous drudgery of a universal history. "There can be no common peace and prosperity without common historical ideas. Without such ideas to hold them together in harmonious coöperation, with nothing but narrow, selfish, and conflicting nationalist traditions, races and peoples are bound to drift towards conflict and destruction. . . . Our internal policies and our economic and social ideas are profoundly vitiated at present by wrong and fantastic ideas of the origin and historical relationship of social classes. A sense of history as the common adventure of all mankind is as necessary for peace within as it is for peace between the nations. Such are the views of history that this Outline seeks to realize. . . . It is one experimental contribution to a great and urgently necessary educational reformation, which must ultimately restore universal history, revised, corrected, and brought up to date, to its proper place and use as the backbone of a general education. We say 'restore', because all the great cultures in the world hitherto, Judaism and Christianity in the Bible, Islam in the Koran, have used some sort of cosmogony and world history as a basis. It may indeed be argued that, without such a basis, any true binding culture of men is inconceivable. Without it we are a chaos."

Mr. Wells has turned to history with the true instinct of the prophet: "I show you", he says, "this enormous prospect of the past which fills a modern mind with humility and illimitable hope." I begin in the last reaches of space, and you shall see that the theatre of our history is a small part of an infinite universe. I begin ages before there is a written record, and you shall feel that by the true scale of time the whole adventure of civilized man is short. Four hundred generations comprise it.

I show you the first human settlements, and the first groping and illogical effort to comprehend the world. You shall feel the persistent presence and also the gradual refinement of your inheritance, the development of language and the arts. I show you the early civilizations of the Nile and of Mesopotamia, and you shall realize the age-long conflict still uncompleted between the conquering nomad and the communities built around the temple and the palace. I show you the merging and separation of priest and king.

You shall learn from history what ideas have held men together and what ideas have made them quarrel. You shall think of the experience of man as one experience, and you shall think of that experience as a process of trial and error in human coöperation. The great imperial designs of Alexander and of Rome, Charlemagne, Jengis Khan or Napoleon you shall study primarily because they throw light on the possibilities and the failures of a great unification. You shall note particularly how men failed here because the mass of them were unprepared to understand their world, how they went wrong there because their sources of information and news were blocked, how great administrative unions have failed because the technique of government was primitive; how rulers defaulted because they were ill-chosen; how necessary is the organization of thought and research to any sane government of affairs. I show you history, not to fill you to the bursting point with patriotic pride, but to make you face consciously problems with which men have always struggled, for the most part unconsciously.

This is the mood in which the Outline should be read. If you pick it up, turn over the pages listlessly, read what Mr. Wells has to say about something you feel you know all about, Greece, for example, or Napoleon or Mr. Gladstone or Buddha, you will probably set the book down with a vast sense of your own superiority. You may not find the perfect account, and you may be disappointed. But if you start at the first page, and read slowly and sympathetically to the last, you will not only fill in vast gaps in your own ignorance, but you will also place whatever you do happen to know in some relation to the rest of human life. That is my experience at any rate. Had I read this book when I was a freshman and again when I was a senior, I should have listened with a little more interest to the professor who lectured about Frederick Barbarossa and Godfrey of Bouillon; I should have had some inkling of who Haroun-al-Raschid was and that Timurlane was not the hero of a rather dull, but prescribed play. Above all, I should not have labored under the delusion that nothing had ever happened east of Constantinople, or that King Louis of France was inspired by the Declaration of Independence.

There must be other Americans almost as ignorant as I am. I recommend this book to them. In fact, I implore them to read it in a humble and an inquiring spirit, to read it with one eye on Washington and the other on Pittsburg, Paris, Moscow and Tokio, to read it thirstily for the refreshment of their souls. I should go further. To any one who will promise to spend the winter reading this book, I should vote to give leave of absence for six months from lectures, committee-meetings, problem plays, and an immediate sense of responsibility for the upkeep of the human race. He will find in it recreation in the literal meaning of that word. He will be helped to see the world as if he had never quite seen it before. He will escape for a time from the blur and racket of a war-ridden soul into the gorgeous panorama of man set in a universe so spacious that for our minds it is infinite, and so old that it is eternal.

He will wonder a little at illusions he has hugged, and hatreds he has nursed, and at the bogies before which he trembles. He will marvel at the little men who imagine themselves immensely practical as they rush about the planet because they scorn to stop and inquire what they are doing and what it is all about. As he contemplates governments and civilizations that have come and gone, he will grow more and more certain that life has not culminated in him, but that it passes through him from a variegated past on towards unbounded futures. He will remember that there have been many sowings and many harvests, that there are more to come, and that the fields in which he labors now will be ploughed and cultivated in strange ways and for strange ends by men much puzzled at his crudity and charitable about his ignorance. A race of men will inhabit this earth to whom our triumphs and our defeats will seem a dim antiquity. They will not remember who strutted the best, or shouted the loudest, or was so magnificent as to put out your eye.

Is that not the beginning of wisdom? And does it not lead, as no other possession leads, to the happiness that only those achieve who in some way are permitted to carry the torch of life? The happiness of creating, and of enhancing, of inventing, of exploring, of making—and, finally, of drawing together the broken, suspicious, frightened, bewildered and huddling masses of men. To be excluded from that happiness is tragic as no suffering and no calamity are tragic. To exclude oneself because of embarrassment and timidity is pitiable forever. It is to have turned away from the light of what Wells calls "that silent unavoidable challenge . . . which . . . is in all our minds like dawn breaking slowly, shining between the shutters of a disordered room."

It is to stumble through life without sharing in the beginning of the knowledge that man can, if he wills it, become the master of his fate, and lift himself out of misery and confusion and strife. He need not forever drift helplessly. He can, if he will dedicate himself to the task in an inquiring and tolerant and reasonable spirit, go a very great way towards closing the gap between his experience and his ideals. For history, though almost every page is stained with blood and folly, is a record also, not perhaps of ideals realized, but of opportunities explored and conquered, by which ideals can ultimately be realized.

It is but a few generations since men first perceived this. It is only very recently that men here and there began to organize deliberately for an increase of understanding. It is but a faint beginning, impoverished, distracted and distrusted. But it is the beginning of a new phase in history, a phase of self-consciousness, in which evidence supplants rumour, research supplants mere accident and circumstance. That is the "dawn breaking slowly," and it will be worth getting out of bed early to see it.

December, 1920

Georges Clemenceau

The desire to stage-manage history is an increasing obsession of our times. But the attempt is usually a failure, even as an illusion, because it is so hard to create illusion when half the audience is behind the scenes.

That, perhaps, is the main reason why Clemenceau's tour left behind it no sharply focussed impression. Few people who stopped to consider the matter believed that the official fiction explained the curious contradictions of the whole performance, explained the Tiger who behaved like a lamb, or explained the coldness of France toward a plea made in behalf of France.

Certainly the fiction as published to the world was not credible. Nobody with an instinct for realities will believe a tale like this: The Father of Victory was sitting quietly in his cottage by the sea. One morning he picked up his newspaper, and there he read that people were saying France was militaristic. He read and he pondered. He thought of Jean Louis the Peasant and the gentle curé of the parish. France militaristic! How terribly untrue. But still he sat in his cottage by the sea. Again on another day he picked up his newspaper, and there in black and white was another terrible piece of news. Rudyard Kipling had told Clare Sheridan that America's soul was lost. He could sit no longer in his cottage by the sea. He must go to America.

America was glad to see him, but it was not prepared to believe in fairies. This old Goth who descends in direct line from Rabelais, Montaigne, and Voltaire was known to have too much of the juice and salt of human experience in him for the role of an ingenue in world affairs. You don't cast Madonna Lisa for Mary Pickford, nor Dr. Faustus for Peter Pan. You don't serve vintage wine as lemon pop, or Clemenceau as Bryan.

The public spectacle was inherently unreal. People gazed upon

63

Clemenceau, and were conscious that they were gazing upon an historical figure. They remembered the legend which has gathered about him, and were glad that they would be able to say they had seen the hero of it. But most of all they tried to realize that he was strong enough at eight-one to undertake an exhausting journey, and this gave them a renewed confidence in themselves. For, after all, political events lie very much on the surface of human life, and to be strong at eighty-one is more significant than all the treaties and guarantees that ever bored and complicated mankind. The vitality of this ancient meant more to the crowds that gathered to watch him than anything he could possibly have said.

What he had to say was certain to be disappointing in the light of his reputation. He was the Tiger who had destroyed eighteen French cabinets, two Central European Empires, and, according to the popular impression, one Wilsonian peace. If he was to seem real in America, there was a very definite Clemenceau character to which he had to conform. People expected to see claws, and instead they were shown a man making a plea so simple that it sounded naïve, and a man who, except for a few flashes which were hardly noticeable, was absolutely scrupulous of all the sensibilities and all the proprieties. Clemenceau's conduct was technically above criticism from the official point of view. His bitterest enemy in France could find nothing on which to hang an objection to him. He kept away from French politics, from American politics, from personalities, and from all practical suggestions. This was perfectly correct and it would have been very dull, if the man uttering these truisms had not been such a dazzling celebrity.

Two interpretations were generally put upon the flatness of speeches. Some people said he was eighty-one years old, and others said that he must be playing some game they did not understand.

The explanation on the basis of age is, I am certain, quite incorrect. If Clemenceau's powers have declined, they must once have been astonishing. For when he was off the platform he was as nimble-minded as men are likely to be, not given to reminiscence or to despair or to hope, but intensely alert to an experience which had taught him always to remember the complications of ambition, and interest, and manoeuver. I came away with the impression that while he undoubtedly loved his cottage by the sea, he liked even better the prospect of battle. And I think he started for America in the first instance primarily because he needed the exercise. It was perhaps a little monotonously idyllic in that cottage by the sea. For Clemenceau has known too many excitements to abandon them voluntarily. He could swear off politics quite sincerely, but so long as he exists, he will have to have just another and just another and just another little drink.

It was some impulse of an old habit like that which at the beginning made him accept the invitations from America. But once a journey was decided upon, it was bound to become a political event. For Clemenceau has been so deeply entangled for fifty years in the mesh of French politics, that he cannot move without causing a political commotion. Intentionally or not his mission at once became charged with the factions and antagonisms of Paris. His followers speculated on what there was in his trip for them. His enemies to the right, the clericals, the militarists, the royalists, Poincaré and Foch and Weygand were on guard at once; his enemies to the left, Caillaux and his friends were infuriated at the prospect of the Tiger's return to public life.

So there broke about him a perfect hell-cat fury both in the ministerial and in the radical press. Why? Because an old man sitting in a cottage by the sea was going to plead the case of France? No, because the most dangerous parliamentarian in the history of the French Republic was again at large. Because the volcano was not after all extinct. Because the Poincaré cabinet, already rotten-ripe to fall, feared Clemenceau to the point of hysteria, feared him most of all because he might be returning to public life as a national figure rather than as a partisan figure.

So in their hearts his enemies wished him the worst of luck when he took ship for America. They hoped above all things that he would be indiscreet. If only he would say something in the exuberance of his oratory which could be described as disloyal! Anything would do, if only it could be made to appear that Clemenceau had lowered the prestige of France or obstructed the Poincaré Government in the midst of delicate negotiations.

The old serpent understand this perfectly. Nothing showed so clearly how thoroughly he was in possession of all his political wits as the flatness and dullness to which he held himself in his American addresses. To be sure he lost lots of applause that he might otherwise have gained, but he was altogether too disillusioned to count applause as an important factor in international politics. He was a genuine realist about his trip. He knew that he could not talk America into a change of policy. No one with his sense of irony could imagine that. He was certain, on the other hand, that the logic of facts would force Mr. Harding back into Europe, and he saw that it would do no one any harm to lend the inevitable a helping hand. He used the utmost political sagacity in that judgment, as events have shown. For the conclusion of his trip coincided almost exactly with Mr. Harding's abandonment of the isolation policy of 1920. And now who will ever be able to prove in France whether his trip was the cause of the change, or coincident with it?

I am inclined myself to think that he wielded a greater influence over here than is generally realized. It is true that people stopped reading his speeches, and probably never read the articles he signed, and that the editorial comment dwindled off at the end. Nevertheless, I think he impressed perhaps a few hundred minds sufficiently to push them over the threshold of their hesitations. I think he influenced the sources of influence a good deal, and helped at a critical moment to make a latent current of opinion overt.

At any rate, in politics, results are more sensational than reasons, and coincidences are almost as effective as consequences. He is returning to France, as this is written, with a record that is officially impeccable, at the precise moment when the chinese wall of American foreign policy has been breached. It is a triumph of luck, if you like, but enough of a triumph to have struck his enemies dumb. They must be calculating feverishly how to counteract the blow which he is able to deliver.

For while Clemenceau may be no man himself to make the settlement which Europe needs, while almost certainly he will not take office again, while his lieutenants may themselves inspire no confidence, the fact remains that in the political game within France, Clemenceau is one of the most dangerous opponents of the militarist-clerical reaction which governs French policy. The ominous silence which greeted his return to France implied no lack of interest. It indicated the fear which the old man inspires.

February, 1923

Alexander Meiklejohn

When he fell, Alexander Meiklejohn had lost the support of all his trustees, of two-thirds of his faculty, and probably of most of the alumni who had never studied under him. Of those who had been graduated during the ten years of his leadership of Amherst College the overwhelming majority are his thick and thin supporters. From the present student body he elicits a kind of devotion which I have never seen before among college men.

I have been with Amherst seniors, leaders of their class, fellows who, in an ordinary college, would be ashamed of their seriousness, and they talk of Meiklejohn as only the greatest of teachers are talked about. I have seen juniors who felt that with the dismissal of Meiklejohn the gates of life had been slammed in their faces. I have talked to professors, trustees and leaders of the alumni. They have a case, a pretty strong case, against Meiklejohn by the ordinary standards of this world, but they were dealing, and in their hearts they know they were dealing, with an exceptional man. They dealt according to the rules of rather common sense with a very uncommon man.

The story of Meiklejohn at Amherst can be told quite simply and frankly. He was born in Rochdale, England, in 1872, and came to America in 1880. His earliest memories are not of New England. He was not educated at Amherst, but at Brown and Cornell. He is married to Nannine A. La Villa, the daughter of an Italian father and, I believe, an English mother. The Meiklejohn household is not a Puritan household.

Eleven years ago it was transplanted into the midst of a very small, deeply rooted New England community. It never took root. It remained exotic and therefore unusually conspicuous. For the President of a New England college is no mere President of a college. He is, by tradition, a lay bishop and a social leader and a first citizen. The Meiklejohns' tastes did not run to that kind of thing.

They had no natural local patriotism, no particular taste for the companionship of some of the local dignitaries; they had an inclination to be bored, and small powers of hiding what they felt.

These aliens came into a community rather more than well content with a fine tradition, used to comfortable living and settled ways. There had been feuds before. At least two other Amherst Presidents within a generation have been ousted. But President Meiklejohn came as a reformer. He came, an alien, openly intending, with the backing of the trustees, to modernize Amherst. That meant changing the curriculum and changing the faculty.

He therefore had irreconcilable enemies from the start. About five professors, it is said, had from the beginning a violent dislike for President Meiklejohn. There is no use attempting to go into the details of this early antagonism. It involved appointments and promotions and brought upon him, I am told, the hostility of one powerful fraternity and the strong support of an equally powerful neighbor. The important point is that Meiklejohn was building a new faculty, and that this meant the shelving and diminution of the old faculty. It means that the President backed the new faculty. It meant a loss of influence, a loss of students, a loss of courses for the old faculty.

An idea of what this meant may be had from the following very rough calculation. In 1922–23 there were in the departments of biology, chemistry, economics, English, Greek, history, philosophy and political science about twenty-seven teachers. Thirteen of these would be rated as new faculty and fourteen as old. There were about seventeen-hundred student enrollments. The new faculty taught about eleven-hundred and the old faculty about six-hundred.

This preponderating influence of the new Meiklejohn faculty seems to have been reached five years ago. But the figures do not tell the whole truth. The intellectual life of the Amherst student body was under the control of the new men. The elite of the student body followed their leadership. Not only in quantity of students, but far more in quality, the Meiklejohn professors had won the students.

Such a change is revolutionary in the life of a small college town. It brings tragedy and jealousy in its train. The tragedy lies in the older men, who had given their lives to Amherst, and now had to watch year by year the students leaving them and giving their devotion to newcomers. The jealousy arose out of this tragedy. Mr. Meiklejohn, I believe, never really faced either the tragedy or the jealousy. He ignored them and tried to muddle through. He failed and that is why he is not now President of Amherst College.

There were two policies open to him. One was to demand at the very start full power to dismiss the faculty. He never asked this power. Probably he could not have had it even when the trustees were still solidly back of him. He could not have had this power, and if he had had it he would probaby have been slow to exercise it, because you cannot turn a large number of old and loyal professors into the street. As one trustee said to me: "Meiklejohn might have built his own faculty had there been a sensible pension system and a plucking board. But without a pension system the ineffective members of the old faculty could not be eliminated without violating the Fifth Commandment." They could not be eliminated without "cause," except as they passed the retiring age, and some of the oldest of the old faculty are not only personally upright and attractive men, but are physiologically fairly young men.

The only other course open to Meiklejohn was to manage the transition from the old to the new faculty delicately and skillfully. He was not skillful, nor wholly delicate, and some of his supporters were wholly clumsy and very indelicate. The fact that the old were old was, I am afraid, rubbed into them. The fact that they were on the shelf was pointed out to them. Differences of educational theory and differences of opinion were identified with the tragedy of the older men and the assertiveness of the younger men. Bitter things were said, and repeated. The old faculty felt their back was to the wall. The defense of the old Amherst spirit became inextricably entangled with the defense of their own position.

What this old Amherst feeling is like and how it reacted to President Meiklejohn is well illustrated by the following letter by Robert Frost, one of the leading American poets and at the time of this letter professor of English at Amherst. Mr. Frost, as it happens, was a Meiklejohn appointee. But this letter expresses what is in the hearts of the older faculty and the older alumni:

69

Dear Mr. Breed:

I am forced after all to give up the idea of speaking at the Amherst dinner, and I owe you something more than a telegram in explanation. I have decided to leave teaching and go back to farming and writing. Strangely enough, I was helped to this decision by your invitation. It was in turning over in my mind my subject chosen for the dinner that I came to the conclusion that I was too much out of sympathy with what the present administration seems bent on doing with this old New England college. I suppose I might say that I am too much outraged in the historical sense for loyalty. I can't complain that I haven't enjoyed the "academic freedom" to be entirely myself under Mr. Meiklejohn. While he detests my dangerously rationalistic and anti-intellectualistic philosophy, he thinks he is willing to have it represented here. But probably it will be better represented by someone who can take it a little less seriously than I.

There are regrets that I mustn't go into here. The main thing is that I am out of Amherst and it won't be fitting that I should speak for Amherst at the dinner.

Believe me deeply sensible of the friendly treatment I have had from Amherst men, and

Most sincerely yours,
ROBERT FROST

Mr. Meiklejohn, absorbed in his task and hating what to him would have been a mild hypocrisy, did few of the conventional things which often mean so much. He did not succeed—I think he did not try very hard—in making the older men personally comfortable. He is not a glad-hander nor, in the college sense, a jolly good fellow. He is personally austere, kindly, humble and diffident.

He is religious but not churchly; he is a patriot but not by Calvin Coolidge standards a 100-per-center. He did not go to town meeting; he neglected to vote. He did not send his boys to the public schools, but engaged tutors for them. He did not always read the Bible in the college church. He is in favor of athletics, but not too deeply concerned about winning games. He brought a spirit into Amherst such as few American colleges have known, but it wasn't, of course, the old Amherst spirit. He was an outsider and, except as to the souls of his students, he remained an outsider. And this outsider was striking and allowing his appointees to strike at the ego of older, deeply planted Amherst men.

Then there entered into the situation something which has not been written about, although it is common gossip at Amherst and fundamental to an understanding of what happened. The Meiklejohn household did not live within the President's income for a good many years. Accumulated debts had to be made good by individual trustees, and finally, two years ago, the trustees read the riot act to him about the management of his personal finances. These finances were adjusted two years ago, and since then no further difficulties have arisen. But this episode broke the moral unity between the President and the Board of Trustees. They did not all put the same weight upon the facts, but it is correct to say, I think, that the trustees believed that from that time on their confidence was shaken. Their minds were now open to the Meiklejohn opposition on the faculty. The natural conservatism of many of the trustees had a specific charge to work on, which made it plausible to believe and emphasize the prejudice against Meiklejohn.

This change in the attitude of the trustees was reflected, I believe, in the faculty. It is reasonable to believe that the opposition became stronger when it was known that the President's support from the trustees was in doubt. It became very strong in the last year. Where formerly there had been three evenly divided groups in the faculty, one pro-Meiklejohn, one anti and one on the fence, there were now two factions only. And most of the neutral group were in the anti-faction. The President was outvoted two to one in his own faculty. He won none of the older men. He retained a majority but not all of his own appointees. How much this was due to convinced differences about educational policy, how much to judgment about administrative ability, how much to belief that the anti-Meiklejohn faction was going to win, I do not know, and it would be invidious to guess.

In any event, during the last winter the faculty of Amherst has been divided into two irreconcilable factions. These factions ceased to vote, it appears, on the merits of a case. They usually voted for the President or against him. There was no middle ground and the deadlock was hopeless. Mr. Meiklejohn was unable to break it alone.

It was on this deadlock that the trustees demanded his resignation. There were some trustees who regarded Mr. Meiklejohn as unfit to be President of Amherst, either because of his personal

71

financial mismanagement or because of his break with the conservative Amherst tradition. There were other trustees, and they were the decisive ones, who voted against Mr. Meiklejohn because, for good reasons or bad, he was unable to manage his faculty. The test for them was his capacity to keep peace at Amherst. He could not keep the peace, he could not command a majority of the faculty, and so they say what else could they do but ask him to go? They point as justification to his final speech, where he said: "I expect to be in the minority, and institutions must inevitably be in the hands of majorities." For they ask how they could have left the institution of Amherst in the hands of one who always expects to be in a minority?

At the end, neutrality on the part of the trustees would not have saved Meiklejohn. One thing only could have saved him. That was a decisive vote of confidence by the trustees. Mr. Meiklejohn asked for such a vote, believing that with it he could overcome the opposition of what was then over two-thirds of the faculty. But the majority of the trustees had lost confidence in him, the decisive minority had not enough confidence to vote unreservedly in his favor. Without a vote of confidence from the trustees the opposition in the faculty was bound to fight harder. There would be no peace. The only alternatives left were active support by all the trustees against two-thirds of the faculty, or the resignation of Mr. Meiklejohn.

Amherst has lost a fine educator and a great spiritual leader of youth because he was an unsuccessful leader of men. He did magnificently with students. He failed with the grown-ups. He could inspire but he could not manage. He was lots of Woodrow Wilson and none of Lloyd George.

Meiklejohn's Amherst was a machine that simply would not work. But inefficient as it was, it produced as remarkable a student body as I ever encountered. Hopeless as it was, it made Amherst one of the most distinguished small colleges in America.

Meiklejohn led grown men badly. Grown men are sometimes a little blind.

June 24, 1923

The perception that the noblest man may not make the best administrator or command sufficient consent comes through in this tribute to Alexander Meiklejohn, a fervent libertarian, a popular

72

teacher, and author of Education Between Two Worlds *and* Free Speech and Its Relationship to Government. *Meiklejohn died at ninety-two, having retired in 1936 as professor of philosophy at the University of Wisconsin.*

[*G.A.H.*]

William Jennings Bryan

It would be insincere to write as if we thought any better of Bryan's career now than we did a week ago. His death does not alter the record; to convert the sympathy we feel for his family and his friends into any sort of pretense that we think he was a good influence upon his generation would be to rob a thirty years' struggle of its meaning. Mr. Bryan had many virtues. He was simple. He was accessible. He was resolute. He had the common touch. But the battle with Bryanism has not been a sham battle. And so as we salute a fallen foe we cannot turn the story of that battle into a farce by constructing a eulogy that no follower of his could wish to hear us speak.

Although Bryan was in national politics for thirty years, he never exercised national leadership. Always he was the spokesman of a faction: when he was a leader he was the leader of one section of the country against another, of one wing of his party against another. That, perhaps, is why he was least influential during that interlude of eight years when the party he had led so often to defeat at last controlled the National Government. Bryan was never so completely obscured as he was during the only Democratic regime that occurred while he was a man of importance. Woodrow Wilson did not make Bryan obscure. He gave him the first place in his Cabinet. And yet precisely when Bryan should have been at the top of his power he faded into obscurity and played no part in the great events of the war and the peace. Astonishing as it would seem, Bryan dominated his party only when it was defeated, and influenced his country least during the greatest crisis of its recent history. It was only when his party had lost control of the Government and was again disunited and the prey of factions that the star of Bryan rose once more.

For he was a natural-born maker and leader of factions. He had great ambition for power, but no taste for the exercise of the power to which he aspired. He espoused causes in great numbers, but he never faced the perplexities of a statesman in office nor made the kind of decision a man of action must make. He was Secretary of State in the Wilson Cabinet, but in those trying days he had neither a plan to make war nor a plan to keep peace. He did not know what to do. Although he was three times nominated for President, he really had no conception of the mental effort required to administer a Government or frame its policies. It was only when he was leading one body of men into collision with some other body of men that he knew what to do. Then he showed genius for uniting a faction by arousing its blazing hostility against some other faction.

It was in these factional quarrels that Bryan aroused such passionate and sincere devotion to what seemed exalted causes. But always the basis of his appeal was distrust of some other group of men. He would preach idealism not as loyalty to a program but as fear of some alleged enemy. With skill and daring and a certain lack of scruple he appealed to the fears which set men violently against one another.

Thus in the course of his career he managed to divide the country sectionally in 1896 and his party at all times when he exercised influence over it. Even in religion he could not refrain from factionalism, and the last years of his life were devoted to a crusade which set one group of Christians against another. He professed himself a Democrat and a Christian, but at bottom he was always a man looking for a point of conflict where his talent for factionalism could find free play. Thus as a Democrat he spent his chief energies quarreling with Democrats, and as a Christian he ended his life quarreling angrily with other Christians.

He understood how to rouse a following and keep it in fighting spirit. But what to do if he won, how to act if he had to act, was not within the range of his mentality. Unless he could find a faction he simply was not a public figure. That is why, in spite of the immense commotion he produced for thirty years, his career was so barren. At the end he was no better equipped for statesmanship than when he began. After thirty years of constant appearance before the American people he had no counsel to give them on their great problems of peace and war. He adopted one "issue" after another, but they were disconnected and casual issues, and whether they were good or bad they originated in no philosophy of government or wisdom about public affairs.

His advice was sought when there was a quarrel inside his party or his church. Then he was always on the scene in full activity. But, except to deepen the quarrel, he had little to offer by way of a solution, for whenever he exposed the inner workings of his mind he revealed merely an odd assortment of prejudices and phrases. He had never bent his mind to the labor of thinking out any of the problems over which he made himself so conspicuous.

It was his conviction that you could solve great questions cheaply, on hunches and by a phrase, that made his influence and his example a dangerous one. The harm he did to his party by committing it against its own tradition to the centralized coercion of Prohibition, the harm he did to pacifism by associating it with empty phrases, the harm he did to Protestantism by associating it with ignorance and legalized intolerance—above all, the great and unforgivable harm he did to his country by introducing a religious feud into politics—were all part and parcel of a life lived without respect for or loyalty to the laborious search for truth.

He had ideals, public and private, and according to his lights he lived by them. But among those ideals there was no love of truth, which alone can render idealism civilized, and no reverence for the method by which truth is attained. At the last this deep defect became overt and Bryan led a crusade against human reason itself. Bryanism ended in what would have become, had he had his way, a religious quarrel throughout the land.

May he rest in peace! And may the Republic whose peace and good-fellowship are threatened by the fires he lighted find peace too!

July 28, 1925

Uncharacteristically, Lippman had few kind parting words on the death of the "Boy Orator of the Platte" and three-time Democratic Presidential nominee (1896, 1900, 1908). Appointed Secretary of State by Woodrow Wilson in 1912, William Jennings Bryan resigned in 1915, in opposition to Wilson's firm response to the sinking of neutral shipping by the Germans.

[*G.A.H.*]

H. L. Mencken

There is now taking place a radical change of attitude not merely towards parliamentary government but towards the whole conception of popular sovereignty and majority rule. This change is as radical in its way as that which took place, say between 1776 and 1848.

In the United States Mr. Mencken is the most powerful voice announcing the change. The effect of his tremendous polemic is to destroy, by rendering it ridiculous and unfashionable, the democratic tradition of the American pioneers. This attack on the divine right of demos is an almost exact equivalent of the earlier attacks on the kings, the nobles, and the priests. He strikes at the sovereign power, which in America today consists of the evangelical churches in the small communities, the proletarian masses in the cities, and the organized smaller business men everywhere. The Baptist and Methodist sects, the city mobs, and the Chamber of Commerce are in power. They are the villains of the piece. Mr. Mencken does not argue with them. He lays violent hands upon them in the conviction, probably correct, that you accomplish results quicker by making your opponent's back teeth rattle than by laboriously addressing his reason. Mr. Mencken, moreover, being an old newspaper man, has rather strong notions about the capacity of mankind to reason. He knows that the established scheme is not supported by reason but by prejudice, prestige, and reverence, and that a good joke is more devastating than a sound argument. He is an eminently practical journalist, and so he devotes himself to dogmatic and explosive vituperation. The effect is a massacre of sacred cows, a holocaust of idols, and the poor boobs are no longer on their knees.

Mr. Mencken is so effective just because his appeal is not from mind to mind but from viscera to viscera. If you analyze his arguments you destroy their effect. You cannot take them in detail and

77

examine their implications. You have to judge him totally, roughly, approximately, without definition, as you would a barrage of artillery, for the general destruction rather than for the accuracy of the individual shots. He presents an experience, and if he gets you, he gets you not by reasoned conviction, but by a conversion which you may or may not be able to dress up later as a philosophy. If he succeeds with you, he implants in you a sense of sin, and then he revives you with grace, and disposes you to a new pride in excellence and in a non-gregarious excellence.

One example will show what happens if you pause to analyze his ideas. The thesis of "Notes on Democracy" is that we must cease to be governed by "the inferior four-fifths of mankind." Here surely is a concept which a thinker would have paused to define. Mr. Mencken never does define it, and what is more, he quite evidently has no clear idea of what he means. Sometimes he seems to think that the difference between the inferior four-fifths and the superior one-fifth is the difference between the "haves" and the "have nots." At other times he seems to think it is the difference between the swells and the nobodies, between the wellborn and those who come "out of the gutter." At other times he abandons these worldly distinctions and talks and thinks about "free spirits," a spiritual elite, who have no relation either to income or to a family tree. This vagueness as to whether the superior one-fifth are the Prussian Junkers or the Pittsburgh millionaires, or the people who can appreciate Bach and Beethoven, persists throughout the book ["Notes on Democracy"].

This confusion is due, I think, to the fact that he is an outraged sentimentalist. Fate and his own curiosity have made him a connoisseur of human ignorance. Most educated men are so preoccupied with what they conceive to be the best thought in the field of their interest, that they ignore the follies of uneducated men. . . . Even William James, who was more interested in the common man than any great philosopher of our time, was looking always for grains of wisdom in the heaps of folly. But Mr. Mencken is overwhelmingly preoccupied with popular culture. He collects examples of it. He goes into a rage about it. He cares so much about it that he cannot detach himself from it. And he measures it not by relative standards, but by the standards which most educated men reserve for a culture of the first order. He succeeds, of course, in establishing a *reductio ad absurdum* of the shibboleths of liberals. That is worth doing. But it is well to know what you are doing, and when Mr. Mencken measures the culture of the mass by the cultural standards of the elite, he is not throwing any real light on the modern problem. He is merely smashing a delusion by means of an effective rhetorical device.

I doubt, however, if he is aware that he is using a rhetorical device. When he measures the popular culture by the standards of the elite, the humor is all on the surface. The undertone is earnest and intensely sincere. One feels that Mr. Mencken is deeply outraged because he does not live in a world where all men love truth and excellence and honor. I feel it because I detect in this book many signs of yearning for the good old days. When Mr. Mencken refers to feudalism, to kings, to the Prussian aristocracy, to any ordered society of the ancient régime, he adopts a different tone of voice. I don't mean to say that he talks like an *emigré* or like a writer for the *Action Française* [a right-wing fascist organization in France], but it is evident to me that his revolt against modern democratic society exhausts his realism, and that the historic alternatives are touched for him with a romantic glamour. The older aristocratic societies exist only in his imagination; they are idealized sufficiently to inhibit that drastic plainness of perception which he applies to the democratic society all about him.

The chief weakness of "Notes on Democracy," as a book of ideas, arises out of this naive contrast in Mr. Mencken's mind between the sordid reality he knows and the splendid society he imagines. He never seems to have grasped the truth that the thing he hates is the direct result of the thing he most admires. This modern democracy meddling in great affairs could not be what it is but for that freedom of thought which Mr. Mencken to his everlasting credit cares more about than about anything else. It is freedom of speech and freedom of thought which have made all questions popular questions. What sense is there then in shouting on one page for a party of "liberty," and on another bewailing the hideous consequences? The old aristocracies which Mr. Mencken admires did not delude themselves with any nonsense about liberty. They reserved what liberty there was for a privileged elite, knowing perfectly well that if you granted liberty to every one you would have sooner or later everything that Mr. Mencken deplores. But he seems to think that you can have a privileged, ordered, aristocratic society with complete liberty of speech. That is as thorough-going a piece of Utopian sentimentalism as anything could be. You might as well proclaim yourself a Roman Catholic and then ask that excerpts

79

from the *American Mercury* and the works of Charles Darwin be read from the altar on the first Sunday of each month. If Mr. Mencken really wishes an aristocracy he will have to give up liberty as he understands it; and if he wishes liberty he will have to resign himself to hearing *homo boobiens* speak his mind.

What Mr. Mencken desires is in substance the distinction, the sense of honor, the chivalry, and the competence of an ideal aristocracy combined with the liberty of an ideal democracy. This is an excellent wish, but like most attempts to make the best of both worlds, it results in an evasion of the problem. The main difficulty in democratic society arises out of the increasing practice of liberty. The destruction of authority, of moral values, of cultural standards is the result of using the liberty which has been won during the last three or four centuries. Mr. Mencken is foremost among those who cry for more liberty, and who use that liberty to destroy what is left of the older tradition. I do not quarrel with him for that. But I am amazed that he does not see how fundamentally the spiritual disorder he fights against is the effect of that regime of liberty he fights for. Because he fails to see that, I think he claims too much when he says that he is engaged in a diagnosis of the democratic disease. He has merely described with great emphasis the awful pain it gives him.

In the net result these confusions of thought are a small matter. It is no crime not to be a philosopher. What Mr. Mencken has created is a personal force in American life which has an extraordinarily cleansing and vitalizing effect. How else can you explain the paradox of his popularity, and the certainty that before he dies he will find himself, like Bernard Shaw today, one of the grand old men, one of the beloved patriarchs of his time? How in this land where all politicians, pedagogues, peasants, etc. etc. are preposterous, has Henry L. Mencken, not yet aged fifty, become the pope of popes? The answer is that he has the gift of life. His humor is so full of animal well-being that he acts upon his public like an elixir. The wounds he inflicts heal quickly. His blows have the clean brutality of a natural phenomenon. They are directed by a warm and violent but an unusually healthy mind which is not divided, as most minds are, by envy and fear and ambition and anxiety. When you can explain the heightening effect of a spirited horse, of a swift athlete, of a dancer really in control of his own body, when you can explain why watching them you feel more alive yourself, you can explain the quality of his influence.

For this reason the Mencken manner can be parodied, but the effect is ludicrous when it is imitated. The same prejudices and the same tricks of phrase employed by others are usually cheap and often nasty. I never feel that in Mr. Mencken himself even when he calls quite harmless people cockroaches and lice. I do not care greatly for phrases like that. They seem to me like spitting on the carpet to emphasize an argument. They are signs that Mr. Mencken writes too much and has occasionally to reach for the effect without working for it. I think he is sometimes lazy, and when he is lazy he is often unfair, not in the grand manner but in the small manner. And yet his wounds are clean wounds and they do not fester. I know, because I have fragments of his shellfire in my own skin. The man is admirable. He writes terribly unjust tirades, and yet I know of nobody who writes for his living who will stay up so late or get up so early to untangle an injustice. He often violates not merely good taste according to the genteel tradition, but that superior kind of good taste according to which a man refuses to hurt those who cannot defend themselves.

Nevertheless I feel certain that insofar as he has influenced the tone of public controversy he has elevated it. The Mencken attack is always a frontal attack. It is always explicit. The charge is all there. He does not leave the worst unsaid. He says it. And when you have encountered him, you do not have to wonder whether you are going to be stabbed in the back when you start to leave and are thinking of something else.

I have not written this as a eulogy, but as an explanation which to me at least answers the question why Henry L. Mencken is as popular as he is in a country in which he professes to dislike most of the population. I lay it to the subtle but none the less sure sense of those who read him that here is nothing sinister that smells of decay, but that on the contrary this Holy Terror from Baltimore is splendidly and exultantly and contagiously alive. He calls you a swine, and an imbecile, and he increases your will to live.

December 11, 1926

The irreverent editor of the American Mercury *and author of* Prejudices *and three volumes on* The American Language, *H. L. Mencken ridiculed the smug, puritanical "booboisie" of the 1920s.*

[*G.A.H.*]

Nicholas Murray Butler

At the end of the twenty-five years during which he has been president of Columbia University we find ourselves in no mood to look back upon Dr. Butler's achievements and to praise him as one who has accomplished his work. It is our impression that Dr. Butler has grown younger in the last few years and that he burns with a brighter flame. As he has grown in influence and in assured position he seems to have less and less inclination to pronounce those high but vague, those incontrovertible but inconsequential truths to which most men of his position devote so much of their attention. He does not merely repeat with unction what other men have thought. He thinks, and he thinks out loud, and he has become one of the half-dozen or so most clearly speaking and candidly thinking figures in American public life today. He has had his reward. In an age when it is the fashion in the highest places to speak much but to say little, and to smother all questions of high principles which can be smothered, he has come to occupy a position of peculiar importance in his party and in the Nation.

His greatest achievement is not the wealth and the expansion and the numbers of Columbia University. These are impressive enough, but in their sheer material bulk they are not without their disquieting features. The great achievement of Dr. Butler is that by his own example and leadership he has cultivated the soul of the university just a little faster and a little more ardently than he has added to its real estate, its endowments and its enrolments. Columbia, for all its size and magnificence, does not, therefore, give off that odor of fat contentment which is so characteristic of the university which has rich alumni, fine buildings, a great football team and no scholarship. The output of learning at Columbia University, especially in the field of moral sciences, is in thoroughness equal to that of any university in this hemisphere; in sheer human vitality, curiosity, originality and boldness it is pre-eminent.

In great measure this is due to Dr. Butler, for in a university the quality of the spirit at the top communicates itself through the whole organization. There was a time some years ago under Dr. Butler when he did not convey to his colleagues that sense of liberation which is essential to all first-rate teaching. Then Columbia languished and lost, where she did not dull, the best that her very best teachers had in them to give. But in recent years there has been a change, a subtle but fundamental alteration of the spirit, which has given to the scholarship of Columbia an assurance and a freedom unsurpassed in American academic life.

The outward and visible sign of this change has been the increasing independence of Dr. Butler in the councils of his own political party. Even those with short memories can remember a time when on great controverted questions the powerful mind of Dr. Butler could almost invariably be found engaged in finding excellent reasons for what his party bosses wished to do. Today these same bosses are worrying about what Dr. Butler is going next to say and to do. There has been a happy transformation from apologist to leader, and by this transformation a notable increase in the dignity of the position which a great university ought to occupy in a civilized community.

Of all the public virtues which are most needed in America today the habit of plain, unfrightened, unvarnished truthfulness is the most important. The old distinctions between Republican and Democrat, progressive and reactionary, liberal and conservative, are so blurred that they mean almost nothing. A sensible man will disdain any of these labels. In the realm of reason the most real distinction today is between those who still believe that thinking matters and those who believe that thinking is a device for rigging up formulas to soothe and bamboozle their fellow-men. The real battle which counts is between the clear speakers and the mumblers, between the straight-minded and the roundabout. And in that battle Dr. Butler is on the front line, and for this above all we are glad to do him honor.

April 21, 1927

Nicholas Murray Butler founded and directed Teachers College at Columbia and was president of the university for fifteen years

83

after Lippmann applauded his "happy transformation from apologist to leader" of the Republican party. Butler shared the Nobel Peace Prize with Jane Addams in 1931 and served for twenty years as president of the Carnegie Endowment for International Peace.

[*G.A.H.*]

Sinclair Lewis

The career of Mr. Lewis is usually divided into two periods: an earlier in which he wrote popular fiction without much success, and a later, beginning with "Main Street," in which he tried only to please himself and had a huge success. Roughly speaking, this second period began with the inauguration of Warren Harding. Mr. Lewis has continued to flourish under Calvin Coolidge.

This is not, I imagine, a mere coincidence. The election of 1920 marked the close of that period of democratic idealism and of optimism about the perfectibility of American society, which began in its modern phase with Bryan, was expressed for a while by Roosevelt, and culminated in the exaltation and the spiritual disaster under Wilson. By 1920 the American people were thoroughly weary of their old faith that happiness could be found by public work, and very dubious about the wisdom of the people. They had found out that the problem of living is deeper and more complex than they had been accustomed to think it was. They had, moreover, become rich. They were ready for an examination of themselves.

Mr. Lewis was in a position to supply the demand. For he too had outlived his political illusions, having passed beyond the socialist idealism of Helicon Hall. At the moment when he sat down to please himself by writing "Main Street," in the heroic mood of one who abandons the quest of money and applause, a vast multitude was waiting for him with more money and applause than he had ever dreamed about.

In this first success there was apparently no element of calculation. It so happened that the personal mood of Sinclair Lewis suited exactly the mood of a very large part of the American people. Very quickly he became a national figure. "Main Street," "Babbitt," and, in a certain measure, "Arrowsmith," became source books for the new prejudices and rubber stamps with which we of the Harding-Coolidge era examined ourselves.

Although we are all endowed with eyes, few of us see very well. We see what we are accustomed to see, and what we are told to see. To the rest of what is about us we are largely anesthetic, for we live in a kind of hazy dream bent on our purposes. For the apprehension of the external world, and of that larger environment which is invisible, we are almost helpless until we are supplied with patterns of seeing which enable us to fix objects clearly amidst the illegible confusion of experience. When we find a pattern which works well, in that it allows us to feel that we have made a large area of reality our own, we are grateful, and we use that pattern until it is threadbare. For to invent new patterns requires more genius than most of us have, and to deal with life freshly in all its variety is much too much trouble for preoccupied men. As a mere matter of economy in time and trouble, we demand simple and apparently universal stereotypes with which to see the world.

Mr. Lewis has an extraordinary talent for inventing stereotypes. This talent is uninhibited, for he is wholly without that radical skepticism which might make a man of equal, or even greater, genius hesitate at substituting new prejudices for old. "This is America," he says in an italicized foreword; "this Main Street is the continuation of Main Streets everywhere." Now a writer without this dogmatism of the practical man, and with a greater instinct for reality, could not have written these words. He would have remembered that the world is not so simple. But what he would have gained in truthfulness, he would have lost in influence. He would probably not have induced a large part of the nation to adopt his line of stereotypes as a practical convenience for daily use along with the telephone, the radio, the syndicated newspaper, and similar mechanical contrivances for communicating with other men.

Mr. Lewis has prospered by inventing and marketing useful devices for seeing the American scene quickly. His psychological inventions are being used by millions of Americans to perceive and express their new, disillusioned sense of America. They are wholly mechanical and they are completely standardized now that they have passed into common use. Because of Mr. Lewis's success in fixing the conception of Main Street, it is now very difficult to see any particular Main Street with an innocent eye. A Babbitt is no longer a man; he is a prejudice.

The art of creating these prejudices consists, in Mr. Lewis's case, of an ability to assemble in one picture a collection of extraordinarily neat imitations of lifelike details. Had his gift been in a different medium he could have manufactured wax flowers that would make a man with hay fever sneeze; he could have crowed so much like a rooster that the hens would palpitate. He has a photo- and phonographic memory with an irresistible gift of mimicry. But since his business is the creation of types rather than of living characters, he does not photograph and mimic individuals. Babbitt is not a man; he is assembled out of many actual Babbitts. The effect is at once lifelike and weird. As with an almost perfect scarecrow the thing is so much like life that it nearly lives. Yet it is altogether dead. It is like an anatomical model of an average man, a purely theoretical concept which has no actual existence. For in any living man the average qualities are always found in some unique combination.

But just because Mr. Lewis's creations are composed of skillful imitations of details, they are extraordinarily successful as stereotypes. The Babbitt pattern covers no actual Babbitt perfectly, but it covers so many details in so many Babbitts that it is highly serviceable for practical purposes. The veracity in detail is so striking that there is no disposition to question the verity of the whole.

It is not going too far to say that Mr. Lewis has imposed his conception of America on a very considerable part of the reading and writing public. To-day they see what he has selected out of the whole vast scene. Now Mr. Lewis is a reformer. He does not assemble his collection of details with the disinterested desire to hold a mirror up to nature. He wishes to destroy what he dislikes and to put something better in its place; he is rarely relieved of an overpowering compulsion to make or break something. Yet this particular zeal is no necessary part of his great talent for mimicry. For he might conceivably have loved life more than his own purposes, and have written a human comedy. Or he might have felt that sense of their destiny which makes all human creatures tragic. Or he might have been filled with a feeling for the mystery that enshrouds so temporary a thing as man, and then he would have confessed that after you have studied their behavior no matter how accurately from the outside, there is much in all human souls that remains to be known. But Mr. Lewis is not a great artist. He has a great skill. He himself is a practical man with the practical man's illusion that by bending truth to your purposes, you can make life better.

There was a moment, I think, when Mr. Lewis was tempted to use his talent with that serene disinterestedness by which alone wisdom comes. I refer to that passage in one of the early chapters of "Main Street" when for the first time Mr. Lewis describes Main Street. Until I reread the book recently I had forgotten that in this early stage Mr. Lewis presents the reader with two quite contrasting versions of the same scene. One is the version we all remember, a dull, fly-specked, timidly gaudy spectacle of human vacuity. The other version, which he soon allows the reader to forget, is romantic, exciting, and full of promise. There is no doubt that at this juncture Mr. Lewis meant to say: What you see in Main Street will depend on what you are; it all depends on who is looking at it. In order to emphasize this notion he gives you first the Main Street which Carol Kennicott sees on her first walk in Gopher Prairie, and then immediately following the identical aspects of Main Street as seen by Bea Sorenson who is just off a lonely farm.

Carol is a comparatively sophisticated person; at least she does not belong to the prairies but to a town which with "its garden-sheltered streets and aisles of elms is white and green New England reborn." Carol, moreover, came from a cultivated home with a "brown library" in which she "absorbed" Balzac and Rabelais and Thoreau and Max Mueller. It might reasonably be objected, I know, that Carol never absorbed anything, let alone such heady stuff as Rabelais. But what Mr. Lewis meant to say is plain enough. It is that Carol came from a background which predisposed her to dislike the raw ugliness of Main Street civilization. And having said that, he introduced Bea by way of contrast and justice to show how delightful Main Street would look to a peasant mind.

"It chanced that Carol Kennicott and Bea Sorenson were viewing Main Street at the same time." Carol looks through the fly-specked windows of the Minniemashie House and sees only the row of rickety chairs with the brass cuspidors; Bea is thrilled by the swell traveling man in there—probably been to Chicago lots of times. At Dyer's drug store Carol sees a greasy marble soda fountain with an electric lamp of red and green and curdled-yellow mosaic shade; to Bea the soda fountain is all lovely marble with the biggest shade you ever saw—all different kinds of colored glass stuck together.

There is a humility in this passage which might have become the seed of a much richer wisdom than his regular practice exhibits. Here for a moment Mr. Lewis used his gift without self-righteousness. Here in this interlude he was willing to show some courtesy to the souls of other people. He was willing even to admit that their feelings are authentic. In this mood, had he been able to retain it, he might have risen above the irritations of his time and his clique, have given even the devil his due, and become the creator of a great American comedy of manners instead of the mere inventor of new prejudices.

But to have done that he would have had to care more about human beings than about his own attitude toward them. Apparently that was impossible for him. He cannot for long detach himself from the notion that what Sinclair Lewis feels about Main Street, about Babbittry, about the Protestant churches is of primary importance. What he feels would have more importance if he had great insight as well as great sight, if he had fine taste instead of sharp distastes, if he had salient intuition as to what moves people as well as an astounding memory of how they look to him when they move. Then his figures might come alive, and been something more than a synthetic mass of detail which serves as the butt for the uncritical, rebellious yearning of the author.

Had he a real interest in character, and not such a preoccupation with behavior, he would have expressed his view of the world through all his characters, and not merely through one mouthpiece. He would have given you Main Street through Dr. Kennicott and Bea and Vida and Percy Bresnahan, instead of giving you Kennicott, Bea, Vida, and Bresnahan through Carol. For that young woman staggers under the burden of the weighty message she is forced to carry. "There—she meditated—is the newest empire of the world; the Northern Middle West . . . an empire which feeds a quarter of the world—yet its work is merely begun. They are pioneers, these sweaty wayfarers, for all their telephones and bank accounts and automatic pianos and coöperative leagues. And for all its fat richness, theirs is a pioneer land. What is its future? she wondered."

She meditated! She wondered! Did she really, or did Sinclair Lewis? I ask the question in no captious spirit. This uncertainty as to who is talking and who is seeing the detail he reports pervades all of Mr. Lewis's books, and prevents him from achieving that "more conscious life" for which Carol yearns in phrases that are borrowed from H. G. Wells. When Mr. Lewis described Bea's walk on Main Street, he remembered for a moment what he usually forgets, that a more conscious life is one in which a man is conscious not only of what he sees, but of the prejudices with which he sees it.

Though he is absorbed in his own vision of things, Mr. Lewis is curiously unaware of himself. He is aware only of the object out there. Carol, Babbitt, Arrowsmith and Frank Shallard have sharp eyes but vague spirits. Mr. Lewis is sophisticated enough to realize how they flounder about, and he laughs at them. But this laughter is not comic, it is protective. It is a gesture of defense by a man who knows that some mature reader, say Mr. Mencken, is going to laugh, and it is better to laugh first. It is not the carefree laughter of a man who is detached from the rather adolescent rebellion which he is describing. On the contrary, he is absorbed by it. Underneath their sardonic and brutal tone, these novels are extraordinarily earnest and striving. "Main Street," "Babbitt" and "Arrowsmith" are stories of an individual who is trying to reform the world, or to find salvation by escaping it.

Carol fusses with "fanlights and Galsworthy," brightly painted furniture, and a separate bedroom. She runs away to Washington but returns to Gopher Prairie, saying: "I may not have fought the good fight but I have kept the faith." Babbitt on his sleeping porch dreams of the fairy child, frets with "veiled rebellions," escapes to the Maine woods, thinks he has been "converted to serenity," isn't, returns to Zenith, and, like Carol, at the end makes a speech: "Tell 'em to go to the devil." Martin Arrowsmith also takes to the woods, escaping from his wife's blue and gold velvet limousine, and at the end says: "We'll plug along for two or three years, and maybe we'll get something permanent—and probably we'll fail."

Dr. Arrowsmith is the only one who may have found what he wanted. He has fled from the barbarians and their gauds, he has left "a soft bed for a shanty bunk in order to be pure. For he had perceived the horror of the shrieking, bawdy thing called Success."

"I am sorry," says Gottlieb when he has to tell Arrowsmith that his great discovery belongs to some one else. "I am sorry you are not to have the fun of being pretentious and successful—for a while. . . . Martin, it is nice that you will corroborate D'Herelle. This is science: to work and not to care—too much—if somebody else gets the credit."

Arrowsmith is saved by embracing the religion of science. But for Carol and for Babbitt and for Shallard there is no religion available which they can embrace, and therefore, there is no salvation. Mr. Lewis knew what to do with Arrowsmith. For there is an ideal in science to which a modern man can give himself and find peace. But there is no ideal for Carol or Babbitt. They would not be helped by "believing in" science, no matter how devoutly. Only Arrowsmith who can do scientific work can be saved by it. Only Arrowsmith finds a god to love whom no man can possess and no man can cajole.

This is the point of Mr. Lewis's greatest insight into the human predicament. There is an unconscious pathos about it, for obviously the religion which Arrowsmith embraces, ascetic, disinterested, purified, is for Mr. Lewis like some fine mystery seen at a distance. That there might be a path of salvation like it for his ordinary characters, though in other ways, is too difficult for him to believe. It would be hard for me to believe. But it would have been possible to put the rebellion of Carol and the yearning of Babbitt in the perspective of an understanding of how, as Spinoza says, all things excellent are as difficult as they are rare. They might have failed, but their failure would have been measured against a spiritual insight as fine as Arrowsmith's. Then at least the author would have understood the failure of his characters to understand themselves.

That degree of insight Mr. Lewis does not attain. He can report what he sees; having known about the religion of science, he was able to report it in Arrowsmith. But in Carol and in Babbitt he was projecting only his own spirit, and when he attempts to make it articulate, he becomes literary and fumbling: "It was mystery which Carol had most lacked in Gopher Prairie . . . where there were no secret gates opening upon moors over which one might walk by moss-deadened paths to strange, high adventures in an ancient garden." Babbitt escapes from Zenith only when he is asleep, when he is drunk, and vicariously when his son tells the family to go to the devil. For Carol and Babbitt are worldlings, and for the worldling there is no personal salvation. He must either conquer the world and remake it, though in that he will almost surely fail, or he must escape into his dreams.

The America of Mr. Lewis is dominated by the prosperous descendants of the Puritan pioneers. He has fixed them at a moment when they have lost the civilized traditions their ancestors brought from Europe, and are groping to find new ways of life. Carol is the daughter of a New Englander who went west taking with him an English culture. In Carol that culture is little more than a dim memory of a more fastidious society; it merely confuses her when she tries to live by it in Gopher Prairie. Babbitt is the descendant of a pioneer; he is completely stripped of all association with an ordered and civilized life. He has no manners, no coherent code of morals, no religion, no piety, no patriotism, no knowledge of truth and no love of beauty. He is almost completely decivilized, if by civilization you mean an understanding of what is good, better and best in the satisfaction of desire, and a knowledge of the customs, the arts, and the objects which can give these satisfactions.

Carol and Babbitt inherit the culture of the pioneers who were preoccupied with the business of establishing themselves in a new world. But for them there is no wilderness to subdue, there are no Indians to fight, they have houses and sanitation and incomes. They have the leisure to be troubled; for they really have very little to do. They have nothing to do which exhausts them sufficiently to distract them when they ask themselves: What is it all about? Is is worth while? Their ancestors came as emigrants, and they divested themselves for the voyage of that burden of ancient customs which, with all its oppressions, made life a rite, and gave it shape and significance. For Carol and Babbitt this European heritage has been liquidated until all that remains of it is a series of prohibitions called morality, and a habit of church attendance without a god they adore or an ideal of holiness with which they can commune. Their religion has become a creed which they do not understand; it has ceased to be, as it was in Catholic Europe, or even in theoretic New England, a way of life, a channel of their hopes, an order with meaning. They are creatures of the passing moment who are vaguely unhappy in a boring and senseless existence that is without dignity, without grace, without purpose. They are driven by they know not what compulsions, they are ungoverned and yet unfree, the sap of life does not reach them, their taproots having been cut. In that great transplantation of peoples which has made America, not many have as yet struck down deep into the nourishing earth. And those who have not are only dimly alive, like Carol, like Babbitt, who are weedy and struggling to bloom.

The "splendid indefinite freedoms" for which Carol yearns are an emancipation from the frayed remnants of the heritage her Yankee forefathers brought with them to America. That stern culture nerved the pioneers to hardship. It merely makes Carol nervous. She will, however, soon be free of this bondage. In the big city, where her creator has preceded her, she will be bothered no longer. She will be a free metropolitan spirit, like Mr. Lewis, free to do anything, free to disbelieve, free to scorn her past, free to be free.

The prophet of this metropolitan spirit, toward which Carol reaches out, is Mr. Mencken. Now Mr. Mencken is a true metropolitan. Mr. Lewis is a half-baked metropolitan. He has just arrived in the big city. He has the new sophistication of one who is bursting to write to the folks back home and let them know what tremendous fellows we are who live in the great capitals. There is more than a touch of the ex-naïf in Mr. Lewis, not a little of the snobbery of the newly arrived. For he has as yet none of the radical skepticism of the true metropolitan. His iconoclasm is merely a way of being cocksure that the household gods of Gopher Prairie are a joke. There is no evidence in his writing that he knows or cares much about the good things which the world city contains, as Mr. Mencken does with his German music, his fine sense of learning, and his taste for speculation about genus homo apart from his manifestations on Main Street. Mr. Lewis is proud to belong to the great city, he enjoys the freedom from the Main Street tabus. But he is as restless in the big city as he is in Gopher Prairie. Unlike Mr. Mencken who is quite comfortable, happy, and well settled, as he shells the outer barbarians from his fastness at Baltimore, Mr. Lewis is forever running about the world and giving out interviews about how Main Street is to be found everywhere. He is probably right for he takes it with him wherever he goes.

The terrible judgments which he pronounces upon the provincial civilization of America flow from the bitterness of a revolted provincial. Mr. Mencken is savage at times, but there is a disinfectant on his battle-ax, because he is in no way turned morbidly in upon himself. Mr. Mencken is not a revolted Puritan. He is a happy mixture of German gemuethlichkeit and Maryland cavalier. But Mr. Lewis is still so enmeshed with the thing he is fighting that he can never quite strike at it gallantly and with a light heart. He is too much a part of the revolt he describes ever for long to understand it. That, it seems to me, is why he cannot distinguish between a sample of human ignorance and the deep-seated evil which is part of this world. Everything is in the foreground and in the same focus, ugly furniture and hypocrisy, dull talk and greed, silly mannerisms and treachery. This makes his books so monotonously clever. He will take the trouble to be as minutely devastating about poor Babbitt's fondness for a trick cigarette lighter as about the villainies of Elmer Gantry. He puts everything in the same perspective, because he has no perspective. Like Carol, he is annoyed by almost everything he sees in the provinces, and all his annoyances are about equally unpleasant to him.

For he is still in that phase of rebellion where the struggle to get free is all-absorbing. Of the struggle that comes after, of the infinitely subtler and more bewildering problems of mature men, he has written nothing, and not, I think, thought much. It cannot be an accident that in his whole picture gallery there is not the portrait of one wholly mature personality, of one man or woman who has either found his way in the new world, or knows clearly why he has not. There are such personalities in America, and Mr. Lewis is not a writer who tells less than he knows, or would fail to draw such a character if he had ever actually realized his existence. But Mr. Lewis's characters are all adolescent, and they express an adolescent rebellion.

Mr. Lewis's revolt against the Puritan civilization had of course to include an attack on the evangelical churches. "That small pasty-white Baptist Church had been the center of all his emotions, aside from hell-raising, hunger, sleepiness, and love. . . . He had, in fact, got everything from the Church and Sunday School, except, perhaps any longing whatever for decency and kindness and reason." This is Mr. Lewis's conclusion at the beginning of "Elmer Gantry," and the rest of the book is a sockdologer to prove it.

Had Mr. Lewis followed the pattern of the earlier novels he would have taken as his theme the struggle of an increasingly liberal clergyman to square his real faith with his creed. He would

94

have made a clerical Arrowsmith. There is, in fact, such a character in the book, Frank Shallard, who symbolizes the central confusion of the churches. But Mr. Lewis merely sketches him in,
and then lynches him with the help of the Ku Klux Klan. He was
not greatly interested in Shallard. His hatred of the Protestant
churches was too hot for any patient and sympathetic interest in
the men who are somewhat vaguely trying to make organized religion suit the needs and doubts of modern men. He is not conscious as yet that somewhere in the ferment of religious discussion,
Carol and Babbitt will have to find an equivalent for the salvation
which Arrowsmith achieves. All that, which is after all the main
question, Mr. Lewis ignores completely. For his central character
he has chosen an absolute villain. And so "Elmer Gantry," instead
of being the story of a fundamentalist like Babbitt beset by doubts,
or of a liberal like Carol, who has more impulse than direction,
the book is a synthesis of all the villainies, short of murder, which
the most villainous villain could commit.

Elmer Gantry is not, however, the portrait of a villain as such.
It is the study of a fundamentalist clergyman in the United States,
portrayed as utterly evil in order to injure the fundamentalists. The
calumny is elaborate and deliberate. Mr. Lewis hates fundamentalists, and in his hatred he describes them as villains. This was, I
believe, a most intolerant thing to do. It is intellectually of a piece
with the sort of propaganda which says that John Smith is an
atheist, and that he beats his wife; that Jones is a radical, and that
he cheats at cards; that Robinson is a free trader, and that he robs
the till.

Mr. Lewis is a maker of stereotypes. He had successfully fixed
his versions of Main Street and of Babbittry on the American
mind. Then, quite unscrupulously, it seems to me, he set out to
stereotype the fundamentalist as an Elmer Gantry. His method
was his old device of assembling details, but in his choice of details he was interested only in those which were utterly damning.
It is as if he had gone to the clipping files of an atheist society,
pored over the considerable collection of reports about preachers
"arrested for selling fake stock, for seducing fourteen-year-old girls
in orphanages under their care, for arson, for murder" (p. 378) and
out of this material had then concocted the portrait of a clergyman. This is a stock method of the propagandist, and one of the
least admirable. There is no truth in it. There is no human dignity

in it. It is utterly irrational. If it succeeds it merely creates new prejudices for old, and if it fails it leaves a nasty smell behind it.

I have seen "Elmer Gantry" described as the greatest blow ever struck in America at religious hypocrisy. It may be a great blow. It may, for all I know, be another "Uncle Tom's Cabin." But it is none the less a foul blow, and I do not think the cause of "decency, kindness and reason," which Mr. Lewis espouses on page 28, is greatly helped by adapting toward fundamentalists the essential spirit of the Ku Klux Klan. The practice of describing your opponent as a criminal ought to be reserved for low disordered minds with white sheets over their heads. A novelist who pretends to be writing in behalf of a civilized life ought not himself to behave like a barbarian.

The animating spirit of "Elmer Gantry" is the bigotry of the anti-religious, a bigotry which is clever but as blind as any other. Were it not that the discussion of religion seems always to stir up exceptional passions, the quality of this book might well alarm Mr. Lewis's friends. For until he wrote it, he had his hatred under control. "Main Street" is a rather sentimental book at bottom. "Babbitt" is pervaded by an almost serene kindliness. "Arrowsmith" reaches moments of spiritual understanding. But "Elmer Gantry" is written with a compulsion to malice as if the author could hardly hold himself. The industriousness of his hatred is extraordinary. He gives himself to an abandoned fury which is fascinating as a mere spectacle of sustained ferocity. You say to yourself: What endurance! What voluptuous delight this fellow takes in beating and kicking this effigy, and then beating him and kicking him again! If only he keeps it up, the sawdust in Gantry will be spilled all over the ground!

For in "Elmer Gantry" the revolted Puritan has become fanatical. The book is a witch-burning to make an atheist holiday.

There has been some curiosity as to what Mr. Lewis would tackle next. Bets have been laid, I hear, on the politician, the editor, the lawyer, the professor, the business executive. It is a fairly important question because Mr. Lewis is a very important man. But what interests me is whether Mr. Lewis will reach maturity, or remain arrested in his adolescent rebellion. After "Arrowsmith" one would have said that he was beginning to be free of that shapeless irritation and yearning which Carol Kennicott typifies. But after "Elmer Gantry" one cannot be so sure. The hatreds are turned inward, as if the effort to escape had failed and become morbid. There is some sort of crisis in this astonishing career, which is not yet resolved.

June, 1927

"Red" Lewis left Yale in 1906 to live in a utopian community founded by Upton Sinclair, and Lippmann's comment on the aftermath of that episode in Lewis' life could have been autobiographical: Lewis "outlived his political illusions, having passed beyond the socialist idealism of Helicon Hall." Was Lewis a realistic reporter of the American scene? Lippmann thought not; the novelist's stereotypes were only "monotonously clever." The first American to be awarded the Nobel Prize for literature, Lewis in twenty-two novels, three plays, and in an imaginery account of how fascism came to America (It Can't Happen Here) was the most widely read debunker in the 1920s and 1930s of a money-minded, complacent middle and upper-middle class.

[G.A.H.]

Walter Weyl

Walter Weyl was identified with *The New Republic* from the late winter of 1913 to the autumn of 1919. Though his personal connection with the paper was always intimate, my impression is that fully half the time he was away on some sort of an excursion to Europe, to the Orient, to Washington on war service, or to his home in Woodstock to write a book. He did not like the routine of an office; he tired quickly of writing articles of the same length week after week; he cared almost nothing for the work of editing, as distinct from writing. He came and went: when he was on the paper his head would be full of plans of the trips Bertha Weyl and he would make and the books they would write, and then when he was away on these trips his head would be equally full of plans for the reorganization and the rejuvenation of the paper. He would come back to his desk in an ecstasy of efficiency and surround himself with filing cabinets and notebooks and memoranda pads. And in about four months he would be telling us that he hoped no one else's plans for a holiday would be spoiled if Bertha and he slipped off to Algeria for the winter.

The organization of *The New Republic* was deliberately based on the theory that none of its editors wished to do much editing, that none of them would remain at their desks forever, and that there would be a place on the board for men who were not wholly organizable. The scheme has defects, but it also has virtues, and not the least of these is that it was the only conceivable scheme under which an incorrigible free lance could dip in for a while to edit or to shape policy, and dip out again without upsetting everybody and everything.

The scheme enabled Walter Weyl to edit the paper as much as he cared to edit it. The arrangement suited him, suited his whimsical activity and his occasional practical fervor, and left him free to indulge his endless intellectual curiosity. It worked, above all I think because he was the most trusting of men where his affections were involved. He was not conscious of personal rights that he had to defend, nor touched by jealousy. I do not mean that he lacked his share of human vanity. He did not. But he was too much interested in a thousand things outside himself to cultivate that sense of not getting what was due to him which is the bane and destroyer of all free cooperation. He was not a good member of a team and knew it, because the work of the team interested him only in spurts. But he was a perfect colleague, nevertheless, because when he was interested he had no personal reservations. There are men who cannot play on a team, but insist on the letter of their theoretical rights nevertheless. There was nothing of that in Walter Weyl. He pretended to no discipline he did not possess. He was satisfied to be a free lance all the time, and when he joined in, it was as a free lance still.

There were no precedents in America for a paper like *The New Republic,* except Godkin's *Nation,* and that was built on one man, whereas the fundamental idea of *The New Republic* was to build on a group. The event which really decided the selection of that group was the Bull Moose adventure of 1912. All of the original editors had been in that affair, Herbert Croly and Weyl very deeply in it. No two books had done more to shape the thought of that period in American politics than Croly's "The Promise of American Life" and Weyl's "The New Democracy." And some day when Theodore Roosevelt's letters are really published, instead of being edited and expurgated in the likeness of the people who hated him in 1912 and admired him only in his last phases, the place of these two books will be more generally known. The evidence will show that they played a decisive intellectual role in gathering up the loose ends of the muckraking era and turning them to constructive use.

It was for the purpose of carrying forward this impulse that *The New Republic* was founded, and it was essential that Walter Weyl should be part of it. He was by far the best trained economist in the progressive movement. He was the only active Bull Moose I ever knew who thought the Progressive program could be justified by statistics of the social facts as well as by moral denunciation. Had the progressive movement survived, as everyone in 1913 thought it would, the work which Walter Weyl intended to do when he joined *The New Republic* would have made a great difference. For he would have played a leading part in the translation of progressive passion into a workable and solidly-founded program. But on the very day that *The New Republic* offices in West Twenty-first Street [in New York] opened for business, the war began in Europe. And by November when the first number was published the Old World of the Bull Moose was shattered. *The New Republic,* instead of pressing forward on the basis of doctrines widely accepted in principle by millions of American voters, found itself suddenly in common with the rest of America compelled to turn its attention from familiar domestic problems to the invention of principles, for which there were no precedents at all.

One's memory of the terrible years from 1914 is full of tricks. We all felt so intensely whatever we believed at any moment that we found ourselves thinking that we had always believed it from the day the Germans marched into Belgium. As a matter of fact, there was hardly a person in America whose attitude toward the war did not change radically as the war dragged on, hardly a person who did not read his feelings at the moment back into the past. There were literally thousands who when the Lusitania was sunk sincerely believed they had wished America to utter a solemn protest in August 1914. There were tens of thousands in 1917 who imagined they had urged America to enter the war when the Lusitania was sunk. By the summer of 1918 there were hundreds of thousands who thought they had always been against neutrality in any form.

If there were not bound volumes of *The New Republic* to prove it, and a row of scrapbooks filled with clippings from the German press denouncing us as hirelings of the House of Morgan and lickspittles of Northcliffe, I should be afraid to say that *The New Republic* was never neutral in thought. But in fact the paper began in November at the point which Roosevelt had reached towards the end of October. It advocated the theory that America should have protested against the invasion of Belgium. We were anti-Wilson and in high favor with the Colonel [Roosevelt]. Walter Weyl and Croly and I spent a night at Sagamore Hill, T.R. as fresh as a daisy at two in the morning, Walter Weyl as alert as ever, and Croly dozing in his chair. But this cordiality lasted only a few weeks. One day the Colonel made an onslaught on Wilson and Bryan practically charging them with personal responsibility for the rape of nuns in Mexico. *The New Republic* said this was not fair play, the Colonel lost his temper, and wrote us a savage letter. I remember how much pleasure it gave Walter Weyl shortly after that to write an article praising Roosevelt for a speech he thought was good.

The quality which we learned to know in Walter Weyl during those times was one that easily lent itself to teasing. I would say, "Walter, what do you think about the armed merchantmen?" Then while he was making a series of dots on his writing pad with a very sharp pencil, I would say, "Yes, I know, you think that on the whole the British view is between sixty-eight and seventy-three percent right." He would like that. It made him feel at home. And then he would begin: "But seriously . . ." and proceed to explain that the British view was on the whole rather more than half right, provided you took into account certain other factors which I had forgotten.

Up in Woodstock one day I asked him how far he carried this habit of statistical judgment. There had been a burglar around, and Walter had just told me that hearing a noise downstairs he had gone down unarmed and carrying a candle to see what was the matter. "You're crazy," I said, "a lot of good your quantitative habits are to you if the best you can do is to offer a burglar a nice bright mark to shoot at." "Not at all," he insisted. "The chances that a burglar would make such a racket were not one in nine hundred; the chances that a door was banging in the wind were as one in four, there being four doors in that room; and the chances of my breaking my neck if I did not take a candle were at least five to one against me."

"And you thought all that out in the middle of the night?" I inquired feebly.

"Yes," he said. "I'm not naturally brave and the law of probabilities is a great comfort to me."

Such men do not make good partisans, I'm not sure they do not make bad journalists. But they make the best advisors in the world. If you really went to him in order to find out if you were right, that is if you did not go to him just to convince yourself more thoroughly, he was the best man I ever met to turn to for help in hammering out an idea. Not only had he read enormously, but he had talked enormously with no end of people. He had a deep sense of fact, and an even deeper instinct for reality. He had that gift which experience itself so often does not give, an intuitive sense of what something distant would be like if you went there and experienced it.

That is why the war was such a personal torture to him when he allowed his imagination to dwell upon what was going on at the front. He could play chess with the war as brilliantly as the best of them, calculate with manpower and casualties, munitions and diplomatic maneuvers. But the human agony which it all meant would make him quiver and give him actual physical pain. Sometimes he could not bear it, the horror would come upon him too fiercely, and he would want to go to Europe and understand so tremendously that everybody would then understand and know how to end it.

There were these two strains in Walter Weyl, that of the intellectual chess player, and that which was almost the artist's gift of complete entrance into other men and a kind of actor's identification with them. When the two strains fused, as they did in his very best writing, he possessed the art of illuminating a difficulty which few Americans of his time could surpass. Oftener the two strains did not fuse, and he would vacillate, now captured by the intellectual difficulties of a question, now enchanted with an alien point of view into which he had lived himself in imagination.

His perceptions were too complicated, and too just, for quick and short journalistic expression. To get the full value of his ideas he needed time and space. The subject had so many facets, all the facets were chapters. Most of the subjects were books. And because he never knew before he started to write whether his intellect and his sympathies had fused, he produced more piles of unpublished manuscript than any successful writer I know. He was the very opposite of the man who prints almost before he is ready to write. Walter Weyl labored prodigiously, and his published material is to the mass of what he wrote and destroyed or filed away as the visible iceberg to the invisible.

And at that he had the external marks of a somewhat indolent person. You could tell that by the ritual he went through spasmodically, such as swearing off cigarettes and planning to take regular exercise. His conscience worked in fits and starts, and things would not get done when they were promised, and books would be half written and abandoned. The pretext for interrupting himself was always excellent. He had had an idea for a play. He had met a man who told him about Chinese history, and he had been reading Chinese history. Somebody telephoned him yesterday evening and he had started to study the eight hour law in Oregon. But actually he interrupted himself because long before he knew it consciously, he knew intuitively that the thing in hand was not going to suit him.

The ordinary ambitions were not strong enough in Walter Weyl to carry him over that dead center of a task where the original impulse is frayed and all the words are dust and ashes. There was no fanaticism whatsoever in him. There was no personal dogmatism. The soul of his intellect was an irresponsible and vagrant play of mind for its own sake, and a capacity for affectionate sympathy with all kinds of people. He had no enemies. He had no, literally no, abiding hatreds. He had no causes, no partisanships, no unalterable commitments. Though at times he could simulate, as in the article on Woodrow Wilson published a few months before his death, a fury out of the Old Testament, there was nothing permanent in his anger and little that was truly himself. He was of the company of Socrates, rather than Isaiah.

He was one of those men who were greater than their work, and who leave more friends than books behind them. Walter Weyl left good books, and the plans of even better ones. But he left more than that to those who worked side by side with him. He left the memory of a mind that was rigorously trained and relentless and at the same time innocent and trusting. There were few dark places in our civilization Walter Weyl had not looked into and realized. He would suffer exquisitely when he heard of pain. But he was slow to reach judgment, and very charitable in uttering it. For even in the tyrant and the bully he saw the complication of motive, and would pause to understand.

1922

Along with Lippmann, Francis Hackett, Philip Littell, and Charlotte Rudyard, Walter Weyl had been recruited by Herbert Croly in 1913 at a salary of sixty dollars a week to edit a new weekly journal, The New Republic. *Felix Frankfurter, a frequent contributor to the magazine, described Weyl as "a wise, sensitive, cultivated and highly civilized social reformer. He didn't think you could save the world overnight, or that, at least, he could do it. He had purpose without being boring about it."*

[*G.A.H.*]

Charles Evans Hughes

It must be delightful to live in a world where all the heroes are on your side and all the villains are on the other. If only the real world of men and affairs were arranged that way, how simple it would all be. Then one could say, as our neighbor the Herald Tribune said yesterday, that the opposition to [Charles Evans] Hughes was inspired simply by "envy, suspicion and trouble-making" and that it was "a symptom of aggravated degeneracy."

But in view of the fact that the real world is rather more complicated, it is fortunate that the President and the new Chief Justice are men of adult mind and that neither is likely to take so naive a view of what happened in the Senate. Both are certain to understand that this protest is a warning of the utmost gravity that the Supreme Court has in the last decade become unbalanced. Discounting all exaggeration in the Senate speeches, the conclusion can hardly be disputed seriously that the prevailing majority of the Supreme Court has been willing to go to very great lengths in vetoing the legislative control of monopolies and in giving to these monopolies judicial protection. A man must be blind indeed not to see that the policy of the majority in the court is the cause of the feeling which is spreading from one end of the country to the other that public regulation has been emasculated by the Federal judiciary and that it is necessary to seek other ways of maintaining public control of public utilities. It is this feeling which is primarily responsible for the insistence of Governor [Alfred E.] Smith and of Governor [Franklin] Roosevelt that the water power of the St. Lawrence River shall be developed by a public authority. This feeling is not local to New York, and it is, we think, no exaggeration to say that, second only to prohibition, the question of how to control monopolies is the most pregnant domestic issue of the present day. A deep and growing sense that the prevailing majority in the court are preventing adequate regulation, and not envy and not suspicion and not degeneracy, is the source of the astonishing protest against Mr. Hughes's nomination. It is our belief that Mr. Hughes is sufficiently the statesman to understand, and in a mood of impersonal detachment to profit by, the demonstration we have just witnessed.

Therefore, if all that we could say for Mr. Hughes were that he has "integrity, wide experience, capacity and intellectual independence," we should feel that we were damning him with faint praise. He would, we believe, be among the first to say that in the Chief Justice of the United States these qualities must, like courage and patriotism in a soldier, be assumed as a matter of course. For the distinctive qualifications of the office transcend such obvious and merely lawyer-like virtues. They call for the very highest art of the statesman, which is to unite the experience of the past with the needs of the present and the future. On the Chief Justice, more than on any other man under our scheme of government, falls the duty, which Edmund Burke described so magnificently, of maintaining the Nation not as a mere "partnership in a trade of pepper and coffee, calico or tobacco," but "a partnership in a higher and more permanent sense"—"a partnership not only between those who are living but between those who are dead and those who are to be born." To maintain a continuity between the deposited experience of the dead, the aspirations of the living, and the inchoate needs of the unborn, to make a Constitution not of mechanical rules but of living memories in which wisdom is the mother of insight, that is the art of constitutional interpretation on which the continuity of the Republic depends.

February 15, 1930

This World *editorial in defense of President Hoover's nomination of Charles Evans Hughes as Chief Justice of the Supreme Court foreshadows FDR's later effort to redress the imbalance on the court by adding justices less disposed to blocking "adequate regulation" of monopolies. Hughes, twice governor of New York, had quit the Supreme Court in 1916 to accept the Republican Presidential nomination. Narrowly defeated by Woodrow Wilson, he returned to public service in 1920 as President Harding's Secretary of State and was the principal organizer of the Washington disarmament conference of 1921–22.*

[G.A.H.]

Dwight W. Morrow

Dwight Morrow entered American public life at a time when all political values were inflated and unreal. The war propaganda had dislocated the sense of truth and had brought into being marvelously effective devices for selling things at more than they were worth. It was the appearance, not the reality, that counted, and the politician, ambitious to succeed, surrounded himself not with the wisest counsellors but with the smartest press agents. It was the function of these press agents to create a fictitious public character for the multitude to gape at, and the utmost care was taken by the politician never under any circumstances to let his private and real thoughts disturb the carefully built-up fiction.

This radical insincerity was regarded in the post-war years as the only practical politics. The effects were devastating. The public man himself became so preoccupied with maintaining his public personality that he tended to lose what personality and what personal conviction he may have had. He became so interested in the "reaction" to what he was doing that he lost sight of what he was doing. Plain speaking and honest thinking being at a discount, the public was fooled and yet knew it was being fooled. The younger generation who first encountered public life in this period turned from it in cynical disgust, and among the people generally there was less faith in the character of the government than at any time within memory.

The historic achievement of Dwight Morrow was that he broke through these conventions of insincerity in public life and raised a standard of intrinsic worth to which men could repair. Like the greatest teachers, he taught by example. When the demonstration had been made as in Mexico and in his campaign for Senator [he was elected United States Senator in 1930 and died a year later], the artificial and synthetic careers which had looked so important

106

seemed inexpressibly tawdry. Morrow did nothing to promote his popularity; it gathered about him from all quarters and from every station in a kind of deep murmur of implicit confidence and deeply felt need. For the rise of Morrow in the esteem of the American people was like an awakening out of a daze of appearances and a rediscovery of the solid, honest substance of real things.

No man of our time has had the complete trust of so many different kinds of people. What were the qualities which made this man trusted in Wall Sreet and in Moscow, at the Vatican and among the Mexican revolutionists, among hardboiled politicians and among star-eyed reformers? Was it because he succeeded in being all things to all men? On the contrary, it was because he based his whole public life on the deep principle that the one common thing to which all the warring sects of man must in the end submit is the truth itself. From this principle he derived the working hypothesis of his career which was to assume that every man was interested in the truth.

He knew quite as well as the most sophisticated among us how often men, when left to their own devices, will deceive themselves and others. Nevertheless, he proceeded on the assumption that they intended to be honest, and by the very force of the assumption made them justify him. That was, I believe, the inner secret of his marvelous successes as a negotiator. By divesting himself of all weapons but these which could promote understanding, his adversary had either to disarm too or feel wretchedly uncomfortable at having to be a deliberate villain. Here at the heart of his power Dwight Morrow had possession of an ancient, mystical insight into human character which the merely worldly can never know. Thus because he touched the deeper chords of their natures, all sorts of men trusted him. They loved him because he had the essential human wisdom which remembers always all the octaves of the human spirit. It is a kind of wisdom which is almost submerged by the raw efficiency of our machine-made ways. He had it, and with it he turned not away from the world to a contemplative religious life, but to the management of the most immediate and practical affairs.

The peculiar genius of Dwight Morrow lay in the fact that he kept a mystical faith in men without losing his own intellectual standards. The commonest outcome of mysticism is muddleheadedness; the visionary can see nothing but the white light of the mystery, and for the rest his speech runs out into rhetoric and his actions into eccentricity. Dwight Morrow kept his mind by using it incessantly, so incessantly that it was sometimes exhausting to others and to himself. He lived at a pitch of mental activity many stages above that of the normal actively-minded man. His brain never stopped going and it never was aimless. It fed voraciously on anything and everything that came within the range of his attention, everlastingly purposeful, endlessly raising questions, forever finding explanations and solutions. He had the incandescence of genius and he never rested.

The acquired character of his mind, as distinguished from its native energies, was formed in the great tradition of English empirical thinking. Dwight Morrow was a genuinely learned man in the field of history, and had circumstances been different, he might readily have been as eminent a scholar as he was a statesman. The history which he knew best was English and American history from the time of Cromwell. This meant that he knew intimately where were the roots of American institutions. Unlike most Americans of the present time, his mind was not severed from the past out of which this nation has come. He carried with him, as something known and understood, the central political tradition of American life, and in his own person he came to exemplify it. Those who have marveled that a successful banker should so quickly prove himself a successful statesman and an excellent practical politician will, I think, find a large part of the explanation there. Dwight Morrow did not come unprepared into public life. He came greatly prepared by the intimate acquaintance of a lifetime with the classic models of statecraft and politics. Thus the things which would have seemed new to an unread novice were through many precedents quite familiar to him.

Because of his loyalty to the Anglo-American tradition, it is impossible in our present intellectual confusion to classify him under such conventional labels as conservative or progressive. In a time when conservatives are for the most part high protectionists he was a free trader by deepest conviction; in a time when progressivism is enchanted with the prospect of regulating mankind from central places, he was a resolute believer in decentralization, preferring the evils of liberty to those of authority. But though the pattern of his thought was the classic liberal view of human affairs, he had no disposition to impose his ideas.

This is, perhaps, the aspect of the man which was most inscrutable to many who watched him. Although he had enormous prestige, it did not interest him to use his influence to promote causes and instigate political movements. Some ascribed this diffidence to his alleged political inexperience. It should really be ascribed to his ultimate wisdom about human affairs. It was this wisdom which made him put relatively small value upon specific laws, arrangements, policies, and the greatest store upon weaving thread by thread the fabric of common understanding. For he was of those who believe that men make institutions, and that all depends at last, not on the forms of things, but on the intrinsic quality of men's dealing with each other.

Thus it was in the art of honest dealing that he was a master, and an example to his country.

October 7, 1931

A successful corporation lawyer who became a partner in the J.P. Morgan Company in 1914, Dwight Morrow was American ambassador to Mexico during the troubled late 1920s. He is credited with re-establishing cordial relations between the United States and Mexico and between the Mexican government and the Roman Catholic Church. His daughter Anne married Charles Lindbergh in 1929.

[G.A.H.]

Thomas A. Edison

It is impossible to measure the importance of Edison by adding up the specific inventions with which his name is associated. Far-reaching as many of them have been in their effect upon modern civilization, the total effect of Edison's career surpasses the sum of all of them. He did not merely make the incandescent lamp and the phonograph and innumerable other devices practicable for general use; it was given to him to demonstrate the power of applied science so concretely, so understandably, so convincingly that he altered the mentality of mankind. In his lifetime, largely because of his successes, there came into widest acceptance the revolutionary conception that man could by the use of his intelligence invent a new mode of living on this planet; the human spirit, which in all previous ages had regarded the conditions of life as essentially unchanging and beyond man's control, confidently, and perhaps somewhat naively, adopted the conviction that anything could be changed and everything could be controlled.

This idea of progress is in the scale of history a very new idea. It seems first to have taken possession of a few minds in the seventeenth and eighteenth centuries as an accompaniment of the great advances in pure science. It gained greater currency in the first half of the nineteenth century when industrial civilization began to be transformed by the application of steam power. But these changes, impressive as they were, created so much human misery by the crude and cruel manner in which they were exploited that all through the century men instinctively feared and opposed the progress of machines, and of the sciences on which they rested. It was only at the end of the century, with the perfecting of the electric light bulb, the telephone, the phonograph, and the like, that the ordinary man began to feel that science could actually benefit him. Edison supplied the homely demonstrations which insured the popular acceptance of science, and clinched the popular argument, which had begun with Darwin, about the place of science in man's outlook upon life.

Thus he became the supreme propagandist of science and his name the great symbol of an almost blind faith in its possibilities. Thirty years ago when I was a schoolboy the ancient conservatism of man was still the normal inheritance of every child. We began to have electric lights, and telephones, and to see horseless carriages, but our attitude was a mixture of wonder, fear, and doubt. Perhaps these things would work. Perhaps they would not explode. Perhaps it would be amusing to play with them. Today every schoolboy not only takes all the existing inventions as much for granted as we took horses and dogs for granted, but, also, he is entirely convinced that all other desirable things can and will be invented. In my youth the lonely inventor who could not obtain a hearing was still the stock figure of the imagination. Today the only people who are not absolutely sure that television is perfected are the inventors themselves. No other person played so great a part as Edison in this change in human expectation, and finally, by the cumulative effect of his widely distributed inventions plus a combination of the modern publicity technique and the ancient myth-making faculty of men, he was lifted in the popular imagination to a place where he was looked upon not only as the symbol but as the creator of a new age.

In strict truth an invention is almost never the sole product of any one mind. The actual inventor is almost invariably the man who succeeds in combining and perfecting previous discoveries in such a way as to make them convenient and profitable. Edison had a peculiar genius for carrying existing discoveries to the point where they could be converted into practicable devices, and it would be no service to his memory or to the cause of science which he served so splendidly, to pretend that he invented by performing solitary miracles. The light which was born in his laboratory at Menlo Park fifty-two years ago was conceived in the antecedent experiments of many men in many countries over a period of nearly forty years, and these experiments in their turn were conceivable only because of the progress of the mathematical and physical sciences in the preceding two centuries.

The success which Edison finally achieved in his specific inventions demonstrated the possibility of invention as a continuing art.

111

Because of Edison, more than of any other man, scientific research has an established place in our society; because of the demonstrations he made, the money of taxpayers and stockholders has become available for studies, the nature of which they do not often understand though they appreciate the value and anticipate the benefits.

It would be a shallow kind of optimism to assume that the introduction of the art of inventing has been an immediate and unmixed blessing to mankind. It is rather the most disturbing element in civilization, the most profoundly revolutionary thing which has ever been let loose in the world. For the whole ancient wisdom of man is founded upon the conception of a life which in its fundamentals changes imperceptibly if at all. The effect of organized, subsidized invention, stimulated by tremendous incentives of profit, and encouraged by an insatiable popular appetite for change, is to set all the relations of men in violent motion, and to create overpowering problems faster than human wisdom has as yet been able to assimilate them. Thus the age we live in offers little prospect of outward stability, and only those who by an inner serenity and disentanglement have learned how to deal with the continually unexpected, can be at home in it. It may be that in time we shall become used to change as in our older wisdom we had become used to the unchanging. But such wisdom it is impossible to invent or to make widely and quickly available by mass production and salesmanship. It will, therefore, grow much more slowly than the inventions which ultimately it must learn to master.

October 20, 1931

Candidate
Franklin D. Roosevelt

It is now plain that sooner or later some of Governor Roosevelt's supporters are going to feel badly let down. For it is impossible that he can continue to be such different things to such different men. He is, at the moment, the highly preferred candidate of left-wing progressives like Senator Burton Wheeler of Montana, and of William Jennings Bryan's former secretary, Representative Howard of Nebraska. He is, at the same time, receiving the enthusiastic support of "The New York Times."

Senator Wheeler, who would like to cure the depression by debasing the currency, is Mr. Roosevelt's most conspicuous supporter in the West, and Representative Howard has this week hailed the Governor as "the most courageous enemy of the evil influence" emanating from the international bankers. "The New York Times," on the other hand, assures its readers that "no upsetting plans, no Socialistic proposals, however mild and winning in form," could appeal to the Governor.

The Roosevelt bandwagon would seem to be moving in two opposite directions.

There are two questions raised by this curious situation. The first is why Senator Wheeler and "The Times" should have such contradictory impressions of their common candidate. The second, which is also the more important question, is which has guessed rightly.

The art of carrying water on both shoulders is highly developed in American politics, and Mr. Roosevelt has learned it. His message to the New York State Legislature, or at least that part of it devoted to his Presidential candidacy, is an almost perfect specimen of the balanced antithesis. Thus at one place we learn that

the public demands "plans for the reconstruction of a better ordered civilization" and in another place that "the American
system of economics and government is everlasting." The first
sentence is meant for Senator Wheeler and the second for "The
New York Times,"

The message is so constructed that a left-wing progressive can
read it and find just enough of his own phrases in it to satisfy
himself that Franklin D. Roosevelt's heart is in the right place. He
will find an echo of Governor LaFollette's [Robert LaFollette,
Governor of Wisconsin and son and namesake of the more famous
Wisconsin Governor, then Senator who in 1924 was presidential
candidate of the Progressive Party] recent remarks about the loss
of "economic liberty." He will find an echo of Governor La-
Follette's impressive discussion about the increasing concentration
of wealth and how it does not guarantee an intelligent or a fair
use of that wealth. He will find references to "plants." On the
other hand, there are all necessary assurances to the conservatives.
"We should not seek in any way to destroy or to tear down"; our
system is "everlasting"; we must insist "on the permanence of our
fundamental institutions."

That this is a studied attempt to straddle the whole country I
have no doubt whatever. Every newspaper man knows the whole
bag of tricks by heart. He knows too that the practical politician
supplements these two-faced platitudes by what are called private
assurances, in which he tells his different supporters what he
knows they would like to hear. Then, when they read the balanced
antithesis each believes the half that he has been reassured about
privately and dismisses the rest as not significant. That, ladies and
gentlemen, is how the rabbit comes out of the hat, that is how it
is possible to persuade Senator Wheeler and "The New York
Times" that you are their man.

In the case of Mr. Roosevelt, it is not easy to say with certainty whether his left-wing or his right-wing supporters are the
more deceived. The reason is that Franklin D. Roosevelt is a
highly impressionable person, without a firm grasp of public affairs and without very strong convictions. He might plump for
something which would shock the conservatives. There is no telling. Yet when Representative Howard of Nebraska says that he is
"the most dangerous enemy of evil influences," New Yorkers who
know the Governor know that Mr. Howard does not know the

Governor. For Franklin D. Roosevelt is an amiable man with many philanthropic impulses, but he is not the dangerous enemy of anything. He is too eager to please. The notion, which seems to prevail in the West and South, that Wall Street fears him, is preposterous. Wall Street thinks he is too dry, not that he is too radical. Wall Street does not like some of his supporters, Wall Street does not like his vagueness, and the uncertainty as to what he does think, but if any Western Progressive thinks that the Governor has challenged directly or indirectly the wealth concentrated in New York City, he is mightily mistaken.

Mr. Roosevelt is, as a matter of fact, an excessively cautious politician. He has been Governor for three years, and I doubt whether anyone can point to a single act of his which involved any political risk. Certainly his water power policy has cost him nothing, for the old interests who fought Al Smith have been displaced by more enlightened capitalists quite content to let the state finance the development. I can think of nothing else that could be described as evidence of his willingness to attack vested interests, and I can think of one outstanding case in which he has shown the utmost reluctance to attack them. I refer to his relations with Tammany.

It is well known in New York, though apparently not in the West, that Governor Roosevelt had to be forced into assisting the exposure of corruption in New York City. It is well known in New York that, through his patronage, he has supported the present powers in Tammany Hall. It is well known that his policy has been to offend Tammany just as little as he dared in the face of the fact that an investigation of Tammany had finally to be undertaken. It is true that he is not popular in Tammany Hall, but though they do not like him, they vote for him. For there is a working arrangement between him and Tammany. That was proved last November when the Tammany organization went to the polls for the amendment which Smith opposed and Roosevelt sponsored. Tammany had no interest in that amendment. It dealt with reforestation hundreds of miles from the sidewalks of New York. Yet it was the Tammany machine which gave the Governor his victory.

I do not say that Mr. Roosevelt might not at some time in the next few months fight Tammany. I do say that on his record these last three years he will fight Tammany only if and when he decides it is safe and profitable to do so. For Franklin D. Roosevelt is no crusader. He is no tribune of the people. He is no enemy of entrenched privilege. He is a pleasant man who, without any important qualifications for the office, would very much like to be President.

It is meaningless for him to talk about "leadership practical, sound, courageous and alert." He has been Governor in the community which has been the financial center of the world during the last year of the boom and the two years of the depression. The Governor of New York is listened to when he speaks. Can any one point to anything Mr. Roosevelt has said or done in those three years to provide the leadership we should all so much like to have had? I do not think any one can. He has carefully refrained during these years from exerting any kind of leadership on any national question which was controversial. That was probably shrewd politics. It has helped his candidacy. But as a result of his strategic silence nobody knows where he stands on any of the great questions which require practical, sound, courageous and alert leadership. And those who think he can supply such leadership next year are playing their hunches.

January 8, 1932

Roosevelt's tolerance of Tammany bothered Lippmann, whereas Al Smith's did not. Lippmann liked FDR's speech nominating Smith for the Presidency in 1928, but was cool to Roosevelt's own candidacy in 1932, as this column indicates. After the election, he endorsed most of the early New Deal, but in the mid-1930s turned against what he regarded as the federal government's dangerous intrusions into the management of the economy. Roosevelt's military and diplomatic measures prior to and through World War II had Lippmann's approval, and he finally concluded that FDR had been one of the twentieth century's three outstanding presidents (the others being Wilson and Theodore Roosevelt).

[G.A.H.]

Oliver Wendell Holmes

There are few who, reading Judge Holmes's letter of resignation, will not feel that here they touch a life done in the great style. This, they will say, is how to live, and this is how to stop, with every power used to the full, like an army resting, its powder gone but with all its flags flying. Here is the heroic life complete, in which nothing has been shirked and nothing denied, not battle or death, or the unfathomable mystery of the universe, or the loneliness of thought, or the humors and the beauties of the human heritage. This is the whole of it. He has had what existence has to offer, all that is real, everything of experience, of friendship and of love, and the highest company of the mind, and honor, and the profoundest influence—everything is his that remains when illusion falls away and leaves neither fear nor disappointment in its wake.

It is impossible for the layman to do justice to Holmes the jurist. But even the layman who has read some of his opinions and has lived among the generations of lawyers whom he has influenced, must be aware that he is one of that small number who have determined not merely the course of the law but the premises and quality of legal thinking. For this great judge is one of the true philosophers of the English-speaking world, and it is the part of the philosopher to show men not so much what to think as how. This is his immortality. He has altered the casts of thought. And not only for lawyers. In the days to come, when only scholars remember the cases he decided, he will live on with Emerson and with William James and with a very few others in whom the American spirit became articulate and ripened into distinction. He has the gift of delivery. I have no doubt that his prose is the purest American writing of our time, and I am not sure but that in the American anthology his wisdom, so firm, so graceful, so spare, so clean, will be cherished as a tonic to the will of man above any thus far uttered on this continent.

It is a delight to honor him, and to express, while he is within hearing, a little something of the esteem in which he is held. He himself, however, has said, speaking more than thirty-five years ago to the under-graduates of Harvard College about the calling of the thinker, what now in the fulfillment of his life should be said of him:

Your education begins when you . . . have begun yourselves to work upon the raw material for results which you do not see, cannot predict and which may be long in coming—when you take the fact which life offers you for your appointed task. No man has earned the right to intellectual ambition until he has learned to lay his course by a star which he has never seen—to dig by the divining rod for springs which he may never reach. In saying this, I point to that which will make your study heroic. For I say to you in all sadness of conviction that to think great thoughts you must be heroes as well as idealists. Only when you have worked alone—when you have felt around you a black gulf of solitude more isolating than that which surrounds the dying man, and in hope and in despair have trusted to your unshaken will—then only will you have achieved. Thus only can you gain the secret isolated joy of the thinker, who knows that, a hundred years after he is dead and forgotten, men who never heard of him will be moving to the measure of his thought—the subtile rapture of a postponed power, which the world knows not because it has no external trappings, but which to his prophetic vision is more real than that which commands an army. And if this joy should not be yours, still it is only thus that you can know that you have done what it lay in you to do—can say that you have lived and be ready for the end.

January 14, 1932

Justice Holmes, who died three years after this tribute (and two days before his ninety-fourth birthday), served nineteen years on the Massachusetts Supreme Court before his appointment to the U.S. Supreme Court in 1902 by President Theodore Roosevelt. For thirty years on the high court, Holmes was an advocate of judicial restraint: "The criterion of constitutionality is not whether one views the law to be for the public good." The opening sentence of his book on The Common Law *had an empirical ring congenial to Lippmann: "The life of the law has not been logic; it has been experience."*

[G.A.H.]

Calvin Coolidge

Anyone who would understand America today must feel in his bones those things which went into making the popularity of Calvin Coolidge. They do not lie upon the surface. Mr. Coolidge does not leave behind him a record of great achievements. He did not shape historic events nor was he a leader in his time. Yet he had a hold upon the American people which has endured, though the successes with which he was identified have proved to be illusions and have collapsed. He touched chords in the American spirit which no other public man of his generation could reach, and evoked a response of feeling which was impervious to differences in ideas, to partisanship, and to changing circumstances.

The quality of that feeling is unlike that which has been held towards any of his contemporaries. Among the great mass of the people he aroused no passionate exaltation, and certainly no great hope. Perhaps it would be accurate to say that Mr. Coolidge reminded the American people of their household gods, and that what he called forth was an ancient piety towards the origins of their life. He seemed to the people to be authentically American, to descend unaltered from the sources of their being. Thus, Calvin Coolidge was not judged by his acts. It was not asked whether his policies had been right. He was superior to his own career because he was representative of at least a part of the oldest national idealism of the American people. He embodied for them, in his countenance, in his voice, in the manner of his life, in his wit, and in his philosophy, the first things of the American tradition.

How this came about, why Calvin Coolidge should have touched the American imagination as he did, would not be easy to fathom. There was a sympathetic communication between him and the people generally, which was unspoken and inarticulate. But it was there. It was this sympathy which outlasted the Coolidge era and it defends him from criticism and resentment at the consequences of that era.

One of the most austere of all American Presidents sat in the White House during the most flamboyant years of American history. It is a strange paradox. Mr. Coolidge typified those very standards of life which his time most flagrantly disregarded. He was for thrift in an age of wild extravagance, for prudence in an age of fantastic imprudence, for caution amidst drunken recklessness. Yet few Presidents have had such easy and such good relations with their people. Mr. Coolidge professed to stand for all the ideals which were being most thoroughly ignored. But the people liked Mr. Coolidge very much and Mr. Coolidge liked the appearance of things, and the irony of this Puritan reigning in Babylon caused no misgivings. The people were in favor of what Mr. Coolidge represented. They were happy in what they were doing. And if there was a contradiction between ideals and practice, it called forth almost no comment. They felt that Mr. Coolidge was right. Few imitated, though most everyone admired, his example.

Mr. Coolidge himself helped to cover up this contradiction. He was firmly founded in his inherited morality, in the simple and consistent beliefs of men who, in the struggle against nature, had learned thrift, and prudence, and resolute faith. He was born into an age when the application of these principles was not obvious; a complex social order had grown out of the early American society. Mr. Coolidge accepted this new social order without question, and assumed that success and failure within it had the same significance as they had had among his ancestors. He was contented with one of the great inflations, and unaware that he was not presiding over an era in which great prosperity was the reward of great virtue. Thus, though his standards might well have made him of all men, a severe critic of his time, a certain unworldliness and an unfamiliarity with the realities of his age and an instinctive trust of those who exercise power, caused him to be untroubled.

That his reputation should have survived the end of his era, and that in the depths of the depression which followed it, he has still a deep hold upon the people, is in many respects a political miracle. It is not to be explained merely by the cynical reflection that the people thought he possessed the magic of prosperity. The more important explanation, I think, is that the people knew intuitively that he presided over but had no controlling part in events. Thus they do not hold him responsible, as they hold almost all the other leading figures of his time. But above all, it is amidst the reckoning that the Coolidge virtues, thrift, prudence, and simplicity, have a fresh significance, and in their mood of self-examination the people have found new reasons to respect the Coolidge way of life.

January 6, 1933

Written the day of ex-President Coolidge's death in Vermont, Lippmann's obituary has a kindlier tone than his earlier comments. For example: "Mr. Coolidge's genius for inactivity is developed to a very high point. It is far from being an indolent inactivity. It is a grim, determined, alert inactivity which keeps Mr. Coolidge occupied constantly."

[G.A.H.]

Charles Townsend Copeland

Nearly thirty years ago when I first came to college, the cult of Copey was already firmly established. It is more vigorous today than it ever was, and to the devotees now scattered throughout all the communities of Harvard men, his seventy-fifth birthday provides a most convenient excuse for a celebration.

What the uproar will seem like to those who have never come within the circle I do not know. To convey to them the quality of the devotion which his pupils feel is like trying to explain to one who never heard him the spell which Garrick cast upon his audience. For the Copey of his pupils is not to be found in works of art, in books that anyone may read, in contributions to knowledge which all can share. He is a teacher who has drawn out of a long succession of pupils whatever native gifts they had for writing in the English language and of appreciating what has been written in English. That is his magic. The conviction that but for their luck in having known him, they would be more deaf and more dumb than they are, that in truth he has helped them to live, is the reason why he is the object of a cult in which there is such fervor, such affection and such gratitude.

The method of his teaching, as it lives in my own memory, seems to me to have been more like a catch-as-catch-can wrestling match than like ordinary instruction. What happened was that you were summoned to his chambers in Hollis and told to bring with you your manuscript. You were told how to read what you had written. Soon you began to feel that out of the darkness all around you long fingers were searching through the layers of fat and fluff to find your bones and muscles underneath. You could fight back but eventually he stripped you to your essential self. Then he cuffed the battered remains and challenged them and shocked them into their own authentic activity.

122

If this description of Copey's teaching sounds a little mad, all I can says is that by the conventional rules it was mad, as genius is so often mad. But in these personal bouts, which were his substitute for pedagogy, miracles were occasionally performed that have placed him among the very great teachers of our time.

He is inimitable. And yet, if I understand the new system which has revolutionized the method of instruction since I was at Harvard, Copey was one of its pioneers. Thirty years ago he was already acting on the assumption that teaching is not the handing down of knowledge from a platform to an anonymous mass of note-takers, but that it is the personal encounter of two individuals. Those appalling clinches in Hollis, those dreaded exposures in the class room, the searching intimacy from which all protection was removed, were in fact a continuing demonstration against mass instruction and the regimentation of learning. Copey was not a professor teaching a crowd in a class room. He was a very distinct person in a unique relationship with each individual who interested him.

And so his reputation grows continually greater, nourished by the gratitude of his pupils and the admiring recognition of his peers. He was already a legendary figure when he was young. He will be a legendary figure when he is old. For the legend expresses a realization by Harvard men that they have among them an incomparable teacher.

April 27, 1935

A course with "Copey," who taught at Harvard from 1892 to 1928, was almost mandatory for aspiring undergraduate writers. John Reed's Insurgent Mexico *was dedicated to him. ("I would never have seen what I did see had it not been for your teaching me.") Van Wyck Brooks, another of "Copey's" students, had this recollection: "A lover of histrionic effects as well as good reporting, he [Copeland] had written a life of Edwin Booth, and, an actor himself as a public reader, he liked young men who were actors too, particularly when they were also very good looking."*

[G.A.H.]

Jane Addams

No one will ever be able to put into words the whole long record of the goodness of Jane Addams. All the world knows that she made of Hull House a citadel of compassion where the dispossessed and the bewildered, the friendless and the forgotten have gone for refuge and refreshment and revival. There is no way to count the human beings whom she helped or to measure their benefits.

Yet if that were all her life has meant, Jane Addams would only stand first in a large company of men and women who in every land and under all conditions are persistently kind to their fellow beings. It is not all. There is something else, which was visible in the beauty of her countenance, was audible in her unaffected voice, is in the style of her writings, and was the special element in her influence. It was the quality within her which made it possible for her to descend into the pits of squalor and meanness and cruelty and evil, and yet never to lose, in fact always to hold clearly, the distinctions that are precious to a maturely civilized being. She had compassion without condescension. She had pity without retreat into vulgarity. She had infinite sympathy for common things without forgetfulness of those that are uncommon.

That, I think, is why those who have known her say that she was not only good but great. For this blend of sympathy with distinction, of common humanity with a noble style is recognizable by those who have eyes to see it as the occasional but authentic issue of the mystic promise of the American democracy. It is the quality which reached its highest expression in Lincoln, when, out of the rudeness of his background and amidst the turmoil of his times, he spoke in accents so pure that his words ring true enduringly. This is the ultimate vindication of the democratic faith, not that men can be brought to a common level, but that without pomp or pride or power or privilege, every man might and some men will achieve again and again the highest possibilities of the human spirit.

It is to renew men's faith, so hard to hold, so easy to lose, that saints are born as witnesses and as examples. Jane Addams was a witness to the ancient American faith that a democracy can be noble, and that serenity and pity and understanding, not merely force and ambition and wilfulness, can pervade the spirit of a strong and of a proud people.

May 23, 1935

Although no anti-feminist, Lippmann seldom wrote about women, perhaps because there were so few in powerful positions during his lifetime. His admiration for Miss Addams is striking, considering how little their lives had in common. She was a suffragette, a pacifist, and a selfless worker among the poor in the Chicago slums from 1889 until her death in 1935. She hoped to "socialize democracy," believing that it was "impossible to set any bounds to the moral capabilities which might unfold under ideal civic and educational conditions."

[G.A.H.]

Theodore Roosevelt

In regard to Theodore Roosevelt, it would be absurd for me to pretend that I can write objectively. As a boy nine years old I saw him, just returned from the Spanish War, on the verandah of a hotel in Saratoga; from that day until that great night in Madison Square Garden when he spoke after he had been shot in Milwaukee, I was his unqualified hero-worshipper. He became for me the image of a great leader and the prototype of Presidents. The impression is indelible and, if I wished, I could not even now erase it. So persistent is it that in any complete confession I think I should have to say that I have been less than just to his successors because they were not like him.

To have captured the imagination of a boy is in itself no proof of greatness and often, when I have admitted the prejudice, friends of mine have challenged me to show that Theodore Roosevelt was more than a glamorous person, and in cold truth an epoch-making figure. It can, I believe, be shown. It is today more evident than it was twenty years ago that his seven years as President were a decisive period in American history.

Theodore Roosevelt was the first President who knew that the United States had come of age—that not only were they no longer colonies of Europe, and no longer an immature nation on the periphery of western civilization, but that they had become a world power. He was the first to realize what that means, its responsibilities and its dangers and its implication, and the first to prepare the country spiritually and physically for this inescapable destiny. The outward symbol of that tremendous awakening is the Panama Canal, which he created because he had the historic insight to see that it was the vital link needed to complete the winning of the west. In the perspective of time this achievement will grow ever greater in its importance because it consummated the building of the nation and marked its entrance upon the stage of world affairs.

This same fundamental insight into the truth that the period of American maturity had opened made Theodore Roosevelt the first President who realized clearly that national stability and social justice had to be sought deliberately and had consciously to be maintained. There were pioneers and social reformers before him, of course, but he was the first President to grasp the fact that justice, opportunity, prosperity were not assigned to Americans in perplexity as the free gift of Providence. He saw that once the period of settlement and easy expansion had come to an end, the promise of American life could be realized only by a national effort. He knew the history of other nations. He knew the pathology of nations—the exhaustion of natural resources, the deterioration of agriculture, the accumulation of wealth and the congestion of poverty, the concentration of power and the concentration of proletarian masses in great cities. He was the first President to awaken the American people to the knowledge that they had come into a time when, to insure a good life for their descendants, they must brace themselves to a new nationalism.

All that has happened to us since he was the dominant leader of the people has been the working out of his prophetic insight. Our mistakes—in the war, in the peace settlement, in the post-war crises—have turned upon the fact that we did not awaken soon enough or completely enough to the responsibilities of our new position at home and of our new role in the world. The mentality against which his whole career was a protest, the mentality of weak and complacent and selfish unpreparedness for responsibility, has been the radical cause of our greatest difficulties. But the historians will say, I am convinced, that Theodore Roosevelt began the work of turning the American mind in the direction which it had to go in the Twentieth Century.

It is not in the battles he fought, in the measures he sponsored, that his immortality resides. It is in this change of direction, it is in this new orientation of the American political tradition, it is in his insight into the imperatives of national policy. Though he did not see all that was in the world or its whole future, he was the first President to see that even for Americans the world is round and that even for them the future is not to be a repetition of the past.

He left to his countrymen, too, a testament in which are the virtues they need most for their new tasks. One was an unremitting sense that American unity is plural, that it can be preserved, therefore, only by a continuing equilibrium among its many regions, classes, interests, and faiths. The famous rhetorical device "on the one hand" and "on the other hand," which Mr. Dooley celebrated so hilariously, was the manifest sign of a profound realization that American unity can never be absolute, rigid, or simple, that it must always be a balance of many interests, each moderately and tolerantly pursued.

Another of the paramount political virtues which he left to the people was that means and ends must not be separated, that they must have no policy which they are not prepared to pay for. One of the cardinal vices of liberal democracies is that they are wishful in their thinking, that they demand many things for which they are unwilling to pay the bills. They are disposed to grandiose policies based on bluffing, to words that are not really meant, to clever tactics and ingenious strategems. Theodore Roosevelt was an inveterate hater of all this, not only because it outraged his sense of integrity but because he had the intuitions of a natural ruler of men and knew that wishful policies lead to disaster and humiliation.

If it is the intangible essence of a great man that survives the longest, like Lincoln's patient charity, it is not unlikely that in the American Olympus, Theodore Roosevelt will become the legendary patron of those who believe that a great people in its great decisions must have the integrity to say what it means and to mean what it says. It is a simple truth—continually and easily forgotten.

1935

The break with TR (recounted in the article on Walter Weyl, page 100) was a lesson to Lippmann not to get so star-struck as to lose objectivity about politicians. Nevertheless, TR was his earliest hero, and sixteen years after Roosevelt's death, he still seemed more than life size to Lippmann.

[G.A.H.]

Amelia Earhart

I cannot quite remember whether Miss Earhart undertook her flight with some practical purpose in mind, say to demonstrate something or other about aviation which will make it a little easier for commercial passengers to move more quickly around the world. There are those who seem to think that an enterprise like hers must have some such justification, that without it there was no good reason for taking such grave risks.

But in truth Miss Earhart needs no such justification. The world is a better place to live in because it contains human beings who will give up ease and security and stake their own lives in order to do what they themselves think worth doing. They help to offset the much larger number who are ready to sacrifice the ease and the security and the very lives of others in order to do what they want done. No end of synthetic heroes strut the stage, great bold men in bulletproof vests surrounded by squads of armed guards, demonstrating their courage by terrorizing the weak and the defenseless. It is somehow reassuring to think that there are also men and women who take the risks themselves, who pit themselves not against their fellow beings but against the immensity and the violence of the natural world, who are brave without cruelty to others and impassioned with an idea that dignifies all who contemplate it.

The best things of mankind are as useless as Amelia Earhart's adventure. They are the things that are undertaken not for some definite, measurable result, but because some one, not counting the costs or calculating the consequences, is moved by curiosity, the love of excellence, a point of honor, the compulsion to invent or to make or to understand. In such persons mankind overcomes the inertia which would keep it earthbound forever in its habitual ways. They have in them the free and useless energy with which alone men surpass themselves.

Such energy cannot be planned and managed and made purposeful, or weighed by the standards of utility or judged by its social consequences. It is wild and it is free. But all the heroes, the saints and the seers, the explorers and the creators, partake of it. They do not know what they discover. They do not know where their impulse is taking them. They can give no account in advance of where they are going or explain completely where they have been. They have been possessed for a time with an extraordinary passion which is unintelligible in ordinary terms.

No pre-conceived theory fits them. No material purpose actuates them. They do the useless, brave, noble, the divinely foolish and the very wisest things that are done by man. And what they prove to themselves and to others is that man is no mere creature of his habits, no mere automaton in his routine, no mere cog in the collective machine, but that in the dust of which he is made there is also fire, lighted now and then by great winds from the sky.

July 8, 1937

The flight to which Lippmann refers was Amelia Earhart's last. On an attempt to circle the world, her plane disappeared on July 2, 1937, between New Guinea and Haviland Island. No trace of it was discovered. Miss Earhart was the first woman to fly the Atlantic (1920), and flew it again, alone, in 1932 in fifteen hours. She was the first to fly solo from Honolulu to the mainland and to fly nonstop from Mexico City to New York.

[G.A.H.]

Newton Diehl Baker

The first time I ever talked with Newton Baker was on a late afternoon in March, 1916. He had arrived in Washington that morning, had left his suit case at his club, and had just returned to his room after taking the oath as Secretary of War in President Wilson's cabinet. He was such a small, soft-speaking, gentle man. It was so queer that he should have been placed in charge of an army during the World War. No one knew better than he how incongruous it was,—that he, the friend and disciple of Mayor Tom Johnson, a life-long reformer and pacifist, should have become the civilian head of the American Army at that moment. "I must begin," he told me, "by signing the orders which will send General Pershing into Mexico."

I thought how strange it all was until he began to talk about Mexico. He talked for a long time, and gradually it dawned upon me that somehow, though he had had only a few days to consider the President's invitation, he had already acquired a most extraordinarily detailed knowledge of Mexican history and of the revolutionary social conditions which had led to Villa's raid and to the existing crisis. How he had learned so much I never found out. For he could not possibly have had the time which an ordinary man would have needed to learn what he already knew about issues so far removed from his personal experience.

Later on, while working for a few months as a member of his personal staff, I came to see that his great gift was a most unusual capacity to select and absorb the data of a problem and to master it intellectually and see it in all its four dimensions. He knew what he was doing at all times. He never seemed to act on guesses and hunches and by improvising; always in important matters he seemed to have a lucid and orderly conception not only of the immediate question but of its history and of what he thought were the

131

lessons of experience. I used to see him frequently, often late at night, during the agitated summer of 1917, and always the calmest spot in Washington was his office. Almost daily he was making difficult and dangerous decisions but never did he seem hurried. Always he seemed deliberate. Always he was judicial. Once he had mastered a problem in his mind, he was able to abide by his own decision with an unworried spirit.

It was this ability to deal with issues intellectually, free of all personal anxiety about the consequences to himself, that made him so great a civilian administrator in time of war. For everywhere it is now known that he was a great Secretary of War, undoubtedly the greatest this country has ever had in time of war. The most serious charge that was brought against him was that he did not develop military preparedness in the year before the United States entered the war and that charge is easily answered. He made, as General [Hugh Samuel] Johnson has testified, the plans for mobilization. But it was Mr. Wilson's business, not Mr. Baker's, to decide how much military preparation there should be while the United States was still a neutral. In Mr. Baker's strictly constitutional and democratic philosophy the Secretary of War must follow loyally the President in matters of high policy just as the soldiers must follow the Secretary of War.

At no matter what cost to himself in the way of personal popularity he was always uncompromisingly true to his understanding of the principles which must govern the relations between an army and the civilian authorities. With unerring lucidity of mind he made his great decisions with full knowledge of what was the business of the Secretary and what was the business of the General Staff and of the commander in the field. He kept the distinctions clear in all matters and at all times, in executing conscription, in his selection of Pershing, in his dealings with Colonel Theodore Roosevelt and General [Leonard] Wood, in the relations with the Allies. He was always simple, always lucid, always definite, and never undecided after he had made his decision.

That made him a great administrator, and the testimony of the soldiers came at last to be unanimous on that point. But he was more than a great administrator. Because he had such thorough grasp of the place of an army in a democratic state, he was able to raise the largest army in our history and then to demobilize it without fastening upon the nation the curse of militarism. It might easily have been otherwise. For almost always in history a victorious army comes home to conquer its own people; the army of Wilson and Baker was quickly dissolved, however, in the civilian population from which it had been drawn.

That this happened was due principally to Mr. Baker's iron resolution taken at the very beginning, that it should happen. Often I heard him say, even at the most critical moments of the struggle, that he was the civilian head of the army, and that he would not forget that after the war there would again be peace. He knew very well that it is dangerous for a democracy to go to war because in winning a victory it may so easily lose its own soul. The great good fortune of this country was that Mr. Baker understood this clearly. And so, if his army did not make the world safe for democracy, it did in any event do nothing to make this country unsafe for democracy.

Mr. Baker, it always seemed to me, had the exceptional strength of an almost selfless man. I do not know of any public man in our time who rose to such heights of power with so little personal ambition, or gave up power so easily and with so little personal regret. He had many enemies, but he himself was almost without enmity. He was one of the kindest, most considerate, and magnanimous human beings of our time. He had no vanity, no resentments, and no sense, I think, that he had been called to a high place at a great moment in history and that he had the chance to carve out for himself a memorable career and a resounding reputation. He seemed, rather, to take a certain satisfaction in the notion that he, who had to send men to the trenches to face mutilation and death, should not, in his place of physical safety, be enjoying the triumphs of his power.

I have always thought, too, and from stray remarks which I have heard him make in later years I feel sure I am right, that the real reason he retired from public life, though he was obviously the heir of Wilson and for long the first Democrat in the land, was that he could not bear the thought of making personal capital out of his career in the war. In 1932 when he came so near to the nomination for the Presidency, he was almost perversely unhelpful to his enthusiastic friends. For in the depths of his spirit there was a humility about the terror of the war and a pity about the sacrifices

133

of the men who had gone to France which made him feel, I believe, that he could exploit no part of it, and that to do anything which brought him profit and glory from it would be unseemly.

We shall not often see a man of his quality, and those who had the privilege of working for him loved him and will think of him as one of the most unworldly men who ever in our time played so great a part in the world.

December 28, 1937

In 1917, Lippmann was an aide to Secretary of War Newton Baker, a former mayor of Cleveland and loyal supporter of Woodrow Wilson. Baker was appointed to the World Court in the Hague in 1928 and was Lippmann's preferred candidate for the Democratic presidential nomination in 1932.

[G.A.H.]

Colonel House

The career of Colonel House was like that of an actor or of a singer in that there is no record left by which posterity can form an independent estimate of his worth. There are to be sure some memoirs, some letters and some papers. But no one who knew the Colonel will make the mistake of thinking that they reveal the man or define the part he played in the history of these times.

He was, in fact, singularly incapable of imparting his own ideas or of acquiring ideas through the medium of written words. He was at ease and in command of himself only when he was dealing with other men face to face and by word of mouth. Those of us who worked for him at one time or another soon learned this; that it was no use sending him a long memorandum about anything. Two well spaced typewritten pages were about the limit of what he cared to take in by reading; the rest had to be filled in by oral explanation. And when he had to write, he wrote very briefly as men do who do not like to write.

Thus the papers of Colonel House are no place to find the man who for so many years, for virtually the whole of Wilson's two terms, was by all odds Wilson's closest collaborator. The work he did was done in private talks with President Wilson and with a small highly selected circle of influential men here and abroad. Just exactly what Colonel House did no one will ever know for certain. For almost all that he did is indistinguishably fused with Woodrow Wilson's career.

That is the way he wished it to be. For he was dedicated to Woodrow Wilson. And that is the way it was. So the man displayed in the memoirs, and even more the man of the post-war legends, is a fiction, almost unrecognizable by those who knew the Colonel when he served Woodrow Wilson.

He was able to serve Wilson because he was in almost every respect the complement of Wilson. The things which Colonel House did best, meeting men face to face and listening to them patiently and persuading them gradually, Woodrow Wilson could hardly bear to do at all. The President was an intellectual, accustomed to acquiring knowledge by reading and to imparting it by lecturing and by writing books. Wilson was annoyed, quickly bored, and soon exhausted by the incoherence, the verbosity, and the fumbling of most talk, especially the talk of practical men of affairs. Thus Wilson liked Newton Baker because Baker had a disciplined mind; his talk was always clear and organized. But Wilson could not listen long to people who said things three times over and always badly, and he shrank from trying to explain his own ideas orally to people who needed to be introduced to them gently. Wilson spared himself personal contact whenever he could, and said what he had to say in speeches, notes, and written memoranda. In order to learn he preferred to read rather than to listen; and when he spoke, he did not wish to be interrupted or to have to repeat himself.

Colonel House, on the contrary, was as nearly proof against boredom as anyone imaginable. Lacking all intellectual pride, having no such intellectual cultivation as Woodrow Wilson, he educated himself in the problems of the day by inducing men of affairs to confide in him. And when he wanted some one to do something, having no authority to command, he patiently and persistently set to work with the intention of making the other man come to feel that he was merely doing what he had always wanted to do.

Thus Colonel House brought to Wilson a faculty which Wilson lacked, though it is essential to a statesman. No one can be President of the United States without having a great variety of personal contacts. And Wilson did not like personal contact, and instinctively shrank from it. Fortunately he knew his weakness, and fortunately he found in Colonel House a man whom he was able to see often without becoming weary, a man whom he trusted and knew to be sensitive and responsive to the things he cared about.

Through Colonel House he remained in communication with men from whom he would otherwise have been shut away. For the Colonel, lacking Wilson's fierce convictions about ideas, had ever so much easier and broader sympathies with ordinary human beings. From this there came, so it always seemed to me, the thing which saved Wilson's administration from the fanatical and sectarian narrowness that is so often the undoing of reformers. The Wilson administration remained until nearly the very end broadly national in spirit, and was never reduced to a factional feud. It might easily have been otherwise, given Wilson's sense of his mission, but for the tolerance contributed by Colonel House.

The Colonel kept open the channels of understanding between the solitary man in the White House and the representatives of all sorts of influential and indispensable men. He kept open the channels with the practical politicians of the Democratic party, men who spoke a language that the President could read but could not speak fluently. He kept open the channels with the parties on the left, with pacifists and socialists and single-minded reformers, whom a President in those days would easily have forgotten about. With equally dexterity he left open the channels of communication with big business and high finance, and with Republican leaders like Mr. [William Howard] Taft and Mr. [Elihu] Root. And, as every one knows, he made personal contact with the leading personalities in Germany, France and Great Britain.

In this fashion he enlarged greatly the orbit of the President's direct knowledge and influence, diminished the opposition, and multiplied his effectiveness. Though Wilson was still protected, as temperamentally he needed to be, he was not isolated. He did not hear only from the people who agreed with him. And because Colonel House managed to give the sense that to talk with him was to talk with the President, Mr. Wilson paid attention to and saved the sensibilities of all kinds of important people that it is perilous for a President to ignore.

Yet from the beginning the relationship of these two men had a radical defect which had grave consequences. Though Colonel House was wholly devoted to the President, though Wilson was not jealous of the Colonel, though the two men had tact, sensibility, and deep affection, the fact remained that the closest adviser of the President of the United States was a private citizen holding no office known to the Constitution. Thus authority was separated from responsibility. The Colonel was more important than any member of the President's official family, and the effect of his position was to place the State Department and the diplomatic service in an ambiguous and embarrassing position. He himself was accountable only to the President personally, and the power delegated to him by the President did much to destroy the efficiency of the Cabinet as the advisers of the President and to accentuate the evolution of personal government in the United States.

In the crucial test the personal relation did not work well though if any two men could have made it work, these two men could have. By force of circumstances the Colonel was compelled at last to emerge from his personal and private role and to become a diplomatic official. When he did, his position within the American Peace Commission [in 1919] and his power to deal with foreign governments became highly confusing. At Paris he was no longer the President's alter ego and yet he was presumed to be more important than his fellow commissioners. When Wilson attempted to negotiate face to face rather than through Colonel House, he found himself playing a part for which he was temperamentally unsuited, a part to which he was unaccustomed. And when the Colonel attempted the role of an official, he did not really know where his authority began and where it ended. For he too was playing a part to which he was temperamentally unsuited.

The tragedy of the peace was due in large part, it has always seemed to me, to the fact that the American delegation, starting with all the aces in the pack, were unable to play their cards. They failed to see that American participation in the League was more important to France and Britain than to the United States, and that their policy should have been to purchase a just and generous settlement with Germany in return for continuing American participation in European affairs. Instead, they consented to a wretched peace, having fallen into the illusion that this was the price they had to pay for European willingness to create a League! They bought the League from France and Britain with a bad peace instead of selling it to France and Britain for a good peace.

This fundamental error, with all its dreadful consequences, may be traced, I think, to the fact that Wilson alone did not have the intuition of a man of affairs, and that Colonel House alone did not have the knowledge of a statesman. It was the composite Wilson-House personality that was so effective in the days of Wilson's greatness, and that composite was dissolved when they went to Paris.

March 31, 1938

"Colonel" was an honorary title bestowed on Edward Mandell House by friends in Texas, whose governor he advised from 1897 to 1904. House was independently wealthy, active in securing the Democratic Presidential nomination for Woodrow Wilson in 1912, and was, as Lippmann says, "Wilson's closest collaborator."

[G.A.H.]

Louis D. Brandeis

The long career of Louis D. Brandeis shows how much one man can do to shape the course of events. In the past forty years it has been Brandeis, more than any other single man, who has kept American progressives from adopting the socialist, as opposed to the liberal, solution of social problems.

I realize how battered an epithet is the word liberal, how it is used nowadays as a disguise by socialists and even by communists, how oftener than not these days it identifies a socialist who has not quite got the courage of his convictions. But, nevertheless, the word liberal is indispensable in discussing a career like that of Mr. Justice Brandeis. And so, it must be insisted that in its sincere and accurate and historic meaning, liberalism is not some half-way house on the road to socialism; it is the exact opposite of socialism both in its ideal of the good life and of the way to attain it.

The socialist would cure the abuses of property by making the government the great monopolist. The liberal would cure these same abuses by destroying private monopoly. He would do this in order to achieve the widest possible distribution of moderate-sized property in the hands of independent and responsible individuals.

To the socialist the function of government is to administer the property and labor of the people for the people's good; to the liberal the function of government is to protect the rights of the individual, among them, . . . the right to own property. For the liberal knows that private property is the solid foundation of personal independence and so of human liberty.

Forty years ago when Mr. Brandeis first became a national figure in the United States, men of good will, men who saw that reforms would have to be undertaken, stood at the crossroad: the choice between socialism and liberalism had to be made. In Europe, those who wished to be progressive took the socialist solution. In this country the tendency among thinking men was to follow their example. And it was at this critical juncture that the example and the teaching of Louis D. Brandeis were immensely influential, it seems to me, decisive.

The matter was tested out in the three-cornered election of 1912: when Theodore Roosevelt and Woodrow Wilson fought their historic battle for the leadership of American progressivism. In that contest Theodore Roosevelt became the exponent, though it was contrary to his deeper instincts, of the socialist solution: he called it the New Nationalism. Wilson took the opposite line, the liberal solution, and called it the New Freedom. In that contest between what we should now call rival ideologies, Wilson's principal adviser was Brandeis. It was from the economic philosophy of Brandeis, and from his immense technical and practical competence, that Wilson drew those leading ideas and those specific measures which made the Wilson reforms liberal and not socialist.

Since Wilson's time American progressivism has had a very different development from European progressivism. For while American social reformers have been and are still predisposed to follow the European path, and to think that to be progressive is to be progressing toward socialism, the immense intellectual and moral prestige of Brandeis has been the greatest single thing which restrained them.

None could dismiss Brandeis as a mere defender of vested wrongs. In any concrete question none could fail to see how great was his command of the facts. Thus by the influence of his example the generation of young men who have come to maturity since the war have been inoculated against the easy acceptance of the socialist philosophy. Many of those young men are now prominent in the New Deal. But for the restraining and guiding influence of Brandeis, most of them, like their opposite numbers abroad, would be socialists. Because of Brandeis, though they have often experimented with socialism, they have never done it with a clear conscience and thorough conviction. He has compelled them to realize the dangers, and so to hesitate; he has kept alive in them the belief that social evils can be cured by the methods of freedom.

This, it seems to me, is the historic contribution of Louis D. Brandeis to American life. In the series of reforms which he sponsored before he was appointed to the Supreme Court, he proved to a doubting generation that the liberal solution was not only desirable but that it was feasible; as a judge he has had a part, though Holmes preceded him, in helping to keep the law flexible enough to permit the liberal solution of the social problem. But his main influence does not, I think, lie in his judicial opinions; it lies in his example and his teaching as a reformer in the prewar era, and in the persistent effect of that example and of that teaching upon a generation of young men.

He has been the greatest anti-Socialist of our age, not in the sense of his being a baiter of "reds" and a hunter of heresies, but in the real sense of his having had a positive social philosophy which is wholly opposed to socialism and is its only true alternative.

The quality and temper of his philosophy can best be examined, not in his own writings, but in the tribute paid to him on his eighty-second birthday by Judge Learned Hand, of the United States Circuit Court of Appeals. For Brandeis does not have the genius of Holmes in raising his ideas to distinguished generalizations: he has been a practical reformer rather than a philosopher. But Judge Hand is like Holmes, a judge who is a philosopher, and like Holmes, he is a master of English prose.

This is how Judge Hand has described the social ideal which Brandeis has held up to his generation:

How does he see the Good Life, He sees it, I think, in terms of the dignity and the independence of the individual, to be secured by deliberately disabusing ourselves of the obsession of bigness. I see his Commonwealth of the Future as a society made up of much smaller units than those we have. The great cities will either have given place to small, or they will be so divided that within their present areas there will be many sub-cities, each self-sufficient. Speed and change will no longer infatuate us: men will be born, will live and die in the same place, perhaps in the same house. The individual will not be a wandering atom without permanent associations or local ties, ever agitated, ever seeking to better himself, ever aspiring to leave off what he is doing in the name of a progress whose pursuit irritates, without satisfying, him. His tentacles will reach out to those about him and grip them hard, as they in turn will grip him.

The fabric of these small societies will be tough: it will not be possible to pull away any part of them without leaving some of its fibres behind and tearing away something from what is left. Reputation will not depend upon manipulated publicity: it will be based upon mutual

141

acquaintance and mutual understanding: each will be judged by those who really know him, and none will be called on to judge those whom he does not know. The individual will not be an anonymity, a number, the empty sign of membership in a class.

Industry will be more genial; among those who have personal contacts, discipline and enforced conformity lose some of their alien and imposed bitterness: the harsh dominion of the machine is assuaged. The industrial units themselves also will be much smaller; for even technologically it is a mistake to suppose that the huge concentrations of modern times are efficient. What they seem to gain in economy of method and eliminating duplication, they lose because their management and even their comprehension pass the measure of men's minds. Responsibility cannot be successfully divorced from continuous touch with detail: in our present aggregations the direction is either without adequate information, or it lacks the initiative which only responsibilty can give.

Amenity and courtesy will be the order of that day, for at close quarters men must learn to live with mutual consideration: one cannot be socially quite intolerable when retribution comes so swiftly. There will be no dominating power, financial or political; individual differences there will be in plenty, but no one will be able to become master. Traditions will arise to correct, to chasten and to inform the hasty and crude conclusions which now sweep resistlessly over our vast undifferentiated societies. There will be no great accumulations of weath, not only because they will be impossible, but because, no longer submerged in a multitude, the individual will be valued not for what he possesses, but for what he is.

Something like this in bare outline is that society in which, I think, he believes that life would be gentle and gracious and noble and free.

This is, is it not, the American ideal of what America is meant to be. And because Louis D. Brandeis did so much more than any of his contemporaries to preserve the faith in the validity of that ideal, historians will call him, I think, the most influential American conservative of his age.

February 16, 1939

President Wilson's nomination in 1916 of Brandeis, the first Jew appointed to the U.S. Supreme Court, touched off furious opposition, which Lippmann, writing in The New Republic, *attributed to "the powerful but limited community which dominated the business and social life of Boston," and which considered Brandeis "un-*

trustworthy because he was troublesome." After graduating at the head of his class at Harvard Law School in 1877, Brandeis made a career as "the people's attorney," investigating insurance scandals and the railway industry, and taking a hand in settling labor disputes. He was on the high court for twenty-three years.

[G.A.H.]

William Borah

The quality of greatness is intangible and hard to define; it must be felt and recognized. But when this quality is present, as it was in Borah, the issues on which men differ deeply do not divide them irreconcilably. So when Borah spoke, the level of the debate would rise at once from the murk of mean contention to the cleaner air of important argument. For it is one of the attributes of greatness to see the issues and to fix them at the level of the enduring truths and the nobler motives which ought to, though usually they do not, control our opinions. It was this magnanimity in Borah that enabled him to fight his battles without inflicting on others envenomed wounds or upon himself the poison of a malicious ambition to prevail.

Thus he is one of those who, like Dr. Samuel Johnson in the history of English letters, are greater than their works. He will long be remembered, and he will be the subject of many biographies, and always the question will be asked why this man, who stood out in his generation with the evident style and attributes of greatness, should have achieved so much less than men of smaller stature and lesser caliber. That same question has often been asked about Henry Clay and about Daniel Webster, and it will be asked again and again about Borah.

In the case of Borah the answer may be found, it seems to me, in a peculiarity of our political practice, in the peculiar fact that Borah could spend his whole life in public affairs without ever having to shoulder the burden of executive responsibility and administrative decision. Borah was never the Mayor of a city, the Governor of a state, or a member of the Cabinet. And so while he dealt with government, he never himself governed. He led a sheltered political life. This gave him a fine independence of thought and speech. It enabled him to maintain intact a conspicuous vir-

144

tue. But it insulated and isolated him from that experience of the hard realities, where ideas have to be translated into acts, in which great men learn to be great statesmen.

The critical period in Borah's life was, I believe, the year 1921 when, having won his fight against ratification of the Treaty of Versailles, his party was swept into power with a great popular mandate to carry on the principles for which he had fought. It would have been natural that Borah, like Mr. Hull for example, should have gone from the Senate to the State Department in order to conduct American foreign relations on the line to which he had committed the country. Had he done this, had he accepted this heavy responsibility, had he had to face in action the consequences of his own ideas, his political education would have been continued. In fact, it did not continue, and so his doctrines, divorced from the reality of specific problems, became dogmatic generalities, and he himself came less and less to understand the difference between making an oration and conducting a government.

That, I think, is why his conspicuous achievements were almost entirely those in which a great speech could stop something from being done. There is no finer chapter in his career, for example, than Borah's brilliantly successful opposition to the crude imperialism of Harding and the earlier Coolidge; the country can always be grateful to Borah for having scotched what was very near to being a conspiracy to invade and occupy Mexico and extend a dollar imperialism throughout Central America. He was magnificently effective when wrong could be dealt with by denouncing it.

But when good could be done only by positive action, Borah remained the orator who believed that the instrument of words, which he used so well, was a sufficient instrument. Thus he was a strong constitutionalist in the Jeffersonian tradition, and this led him to oppose the anti-lynching bill. But it did not prevent him from giving passionate support to the Eighteenth Amendment, because here, the evil of the saloon seemed to him so tremendous that he would never appreciate the moral corruption caused by the difficulty of enforcing Federal prohibition.

He hated war as he hated the saloon, and for years he believed that if war were "outlawed" by denouncing it, wars would cease. He hated monopoly; so he denounced monopoly and called on the Executive to enforce the laws against monopoly. But he would never seriously consider the problem of the men in the Department of Justice who had actually to enforce the laws against monopoly. . . .

There was never a question of his sincerity. He had a superb sincerity. Nor of his integrity; he was scrupulous to a point which few men of his time could match. But he was a victim of the fact that he was never anything but a Senator, and could, therefore, voice his convictions without having to bear the practical responsibility for them.

The latter years of his public life were, it seemed to me, saddened by the realization, which he could not conceal from himself, that the world was not the kind of place he had hoped and imagined it to be. Borah was an isolationist from Europe; but what made him an isolationist in 1919, after he had advocated participation in the war, was a deep feeling of moral outrage against the betrayals and injustices of the Treaty of Versailles. Borah was not an isolationist in the sense that he was indifferent to moral issues in the rest of the world. He hated tyranny and evil as Americans of the great tradition have always hated it; he was an isolationist out of the generosity of his spirit, because he loved liberty and believed, as Archibald Macleish has so eloquently put it, that America is a promise to the people and that "when the time came they would speak and the rest would listen."

To this mystic chord in Borah those who have breathed the American air responded, and that is why his limitations as a statesman do not obscure his great qualities as a man.

January 23, 1940

As shown in this generous estimate of the man from Idaho who remained in the U.S. Senate from 1906 until his death in 1940 and was chairman of its Foreign Relations Committee from 1924 to 1933, Lippmann and Senator George Norris disagreed about William Borah. Norris said that Borah "fights until he sees the whites of their eyes."

[*G.A.H.*]

Woodrow Wilson

The fame of Woodrow Wilson is still unsettled in the American tradition, and not we, but at the earliest our successors, will know his story. There is nothing unusual in that. Mr. Justice Holmes, who fought under Lincoln, used to say that not until twenty years after the war had ended, when at last it was certain that the Union had in fact been preserved, and when we had read the Lincoln papers, did he realize that Lincoln was a great man. How, then, can we hope now to appraise Wilson—when the great struggle of the twentieth century is still undecided, now when the work which he began, of finding the true place of America in the ordered community of mankind, is still in its first beginnings?

Yet whatever the verdict of history, of one thing we may be sure: the fame of Wilson is bound up with our own fate, and what Americans think of him in the years to come will hang upon whether we win or lose, succeed or fail. Washington would not be revered as the father of his country if those who followed him had not made a nation which could look back to him with reverence, and Lincoln would not be in glory if the Union which he maintained had not flourished. Thus we cannot appraise Woodrow Wilson. But we must instead regard him, though dead, as our contemporary, and think of him as a general who lost a battle but not the war, and seek humbly to learn from his experience.

This is not easy. For we are too close to the enormous event to measure it clearly, but we can try to find a few bits and pieces, perhaps, of the truth.

Woodrow Wilson left behind him a country which was divided between those who swore by him as a prophet and those who firmly believed that his ideals were a threat to the integrity and independence of the country. Was this controversy which wracked us and paralyzed us for a generation a real and irreconcilable issue; I venture to think it was not, and that it arose originally from the fact that Wilson chose mistakenly to state his war aims in the language of a philanthropic crusade. He told the people what they ought to fight for, but he shrank from telling them prosaically why in fact they were compelled to fight.

Though in reality we went to war in 1917 because the vital security of the western hemisphere was threatened by the imminent collapse of France and the submarine blockade of Great Britain, he never made this clear. As a result Americans never understood why they went to war when they did go: thus a whole generation never really understood our victory because they did not realize the peril it had averted. Not realizing the peril, the reason for a league to prevent war was not clear, and the league was presented to them not as a measure of vital interest to American security but as an irrational duty to "intervene" in the irrelevant wars of foreign nations.

A second grievous error which Wilson made was in failing to make agreements with the Allies prior to the Armistice. He thought that by announcing his own principles of settlement on the great disputed boundary questions, and then by obtaining a surrender from the enemy on those terms, that his own terms would be generally binding. They were not. For in not consulting the Allies, in not negotiating agreements with them, in not talking to them and with them but in talking over the heads of governments to the anonymous masses of the peoples everywhere, he ran into difficulties at the Paris conference which he was never able to surmount.

These difficulties led him to a third mistake which proved, I think, to be the final and fatal mistake.

His task at Paris was to bring about a European settlement which could be maintained and peaceably modified with moderate and occasional, not a great and continuous, American intervention as a member of the League of Nations. To accomplish this he needed a settlement of European questions which rested largely on consent and at that time—the situation today is perhaps radically different—a settlement by consent depended upon fixing terms for Germany which were workable and were morally unassailable because they were in accord with the engagements made in the Armistice.

But as it transpired that unworkable terms, especially in the matter of reparations, were going to be demanded, and that the moral obligations of the Armistice were to be broken, Wilson made the immense miscalculation of thinking that if he could get the league, the vices of the settlement could eventually be cured. Because he thought this, he agreed to the vices of the treaty in return for European acceptance of the league, having failed to see that he should have done just the opposite—namely, to insist that a better and more loyal treaty was the condition upon which America could participate in the league.

Thus when he came home with the bad treaty and the good league, he found that the more Americans examined the treaty, the less they wanted to join the league which was to enforce it. This, and not the machinations of Henry Cabot Lodge, is what really turned the tide of American opinion against the league.

When opinion had turned, and with no understanding of why America had had to fight the war and, therefore, of why a world order was a vital American interest, it came about that on top of all that, no systematic plan of demobilization existed to deal with the human consequences of the war. Then there was fomented a great revulsion of feeling. It was a revulsion against the war, against war, against all that Wilson had stood for, against our Allies, against armaments, alliances and strategic defense—against every element of a sound national policy—and the country passed into the disillusioned lethargy which led us unprepared and not alert to Pearl Harbor.

So what Woodrow Wilson began remains more than ever to be done. For what he sought, which was to discover and to accomplish the American destiny in the twentieth century, is the work upon which we are engaged. It is so great a work we can do no more than to hope to carry it forward a bit—and then only if we are as wise as our young men have shown themselves to be brave—forward to a place where they can carry it further.

December 26, 1942

149

William Allen White

In the town of Emporia in the State of Kansas there died on Saturday one of the most widely beloved Americans of our time. Yet for nearly fifty years he said what was in his mind so that none could misunderstand where he stood on the greatest issues which have aroused our people; and again and again he was a crusader for his convictions. It was not then by hiding his opinions for fear of offending those who disagreed with him that he won and held the affectionate confidence of men and women in every walk of life and of every faction and every sect.

Will White was loved because he did in fact give unto others that which they were then irresistibly drawn to give back to him, and would have been uncomfortably ashamed not to give back to him. He liked them enough to enjoy them. He liked, and he had the eye of a poet to discern, that thing in each other man which, when all the tumult and the shouting are over, is still the best thing the other man is and could be. And to this, because modern men are lonely in their souls and are hungry for fellowship, his countrymen responded, and they laughed with him at themselves and at him with themselves, and felt comforted and were made whole again.

His life is the proof that democracy is more than a method of government, and more than a bill of rights and more than the liberties and equalities of men. It is a fraternity which holds men together against anything that could divide them. It cools their fevers, subdues their appetites and restrains them from believing and saying and doing those irreconcilable, irreparable, inexpiable things which burst asunder the bonds of affection and of trust.

Will White was a gifted writer, a shrewd politician, a fascinating person and something of a prophet. But what made him the greatest single influence for good in the journalism and in the public life of our age was that he was an example of how a free citizen can be entirely independent within the community of his fellow men. He could not and would not become separated from them. He was never crabbed, envenomed, fanatical because he felt instinctively and knew by experience, that the community must go on, and indeed will go on, no matter who wins the argument, who carries the election, who has triumph and who the disappointment. This is the positive virtue of which tolerance is only the negative aspect. And this is the true patriotism of a democracy—that a man should, as William Allen White did, love his countrymen along with his country.

All my life, since I first became aware of anything, I have known him and, like countless others, have leaned upon him as younger men do upon older men. He was something to lean upon, far solider and more genuine than the enumerated abstractions and the series of generalities by which we have sought to express the democratic faith in this age when faith had become dim and the faith is challenged. For as long as I can remember when any one wished to find out or was advising some one from abroad how to find out what was the American view at the heart of the nation and in its purest form, he turned as a matter of course to William Allen White in Emporia, Kan.

Yet he was no more the average or the typical American than was Lincoln or than Churchill is the average and typical Englishman. He was a representative man who could have been only an American, could have matured only on this soil and in this tradition. But he was not the composite average of the American qualities, the good and the bad; he represented what these varied qualities are meant to be and are capable of being. That is why he touched men's hearts. For they felt that somehow he was something of which they who live on the same soil and in the same tradition were meant to be.

February 1, 1944

The most widely publicized editorial of the Pulitzer prize-winning "Sage of Emporia" and internationally minded rural Republican was "What's Wrong with Kansas," written by William Allen White in 1896. It blasted the populists of the day and championed the Presidential ambitions of William McKinley. White abandoned his Republican regularity, however, when he bolted to

Theodore Roosevelt and the Progressive third party in 1912. He was the author of biographies of Woodrow Wilson and Calvin Coolidge, an autobiography, and several novels. Lippmann's column was written two days after White's death at seventy-five.

[G.A.H.]

Henry Wallace

Mr. Wallace is subject to a test such as no other candidate for Vice-President has ever before had to meet. He is treated as if he were a candidate for President. One has only to compare his position with that of Governor [John] Bricker [of Ohio] who was nominated on the general assumption that there is no normal probability of his becoming President. If the country thought that there was a serious possibility of his being President, there is little doubt that virtually all but the rank and file of the habitual Republicans would bolt the ticket. In so far as Governor Bricker is accepted by independents who would prefer to vote Republican, it is on the notion that they are voting not for another Harding but for a Throttlebottom [the fictional vice presidential candidate in George and Ira Gershwin's musical comedy, *Of Thee I Sing*].

But Mr. Wallace is no Throttlebottom, and the question of his renomination is by general understanding the question of visualizing him as President of the United States.

On one thing all will agree. Mr. Wallace arouses intense, almost fanatical, partisanship. His friends, who are legion, give him the kind of devotion which Bryan and the elder LaFollete in their day aroused. His enemies, who are also legion, are irreconcilable. The fundamental question before the Democratic convention is whether, with the President running for a fourth term, they can nominate a Vice-President, not unlikely to be President in this fourth term, who divides the people so deeply and so sharply.

This is a consideration which transcends not only personalities but even specific issues. The case for the President's re-election must perforce be based on the argument that the complicated machinery of war-making and peace-making would become seriously stalled by a change of administration. But this argument is bound to falter if the country sees a serious possibility that this complicated machine might pass into the hands of a man who, regardless of his high qualities of mind and heart, divides the country.

The matter ought not, it seems to me, to be presented as a factional quarrel in which Henry Wallace wins and is triumphant or loses and is humiliated. His own conscience, which is as disinterested as that of any man in our public life, must tell him that in these times, with the great things that are at stake, a man who divides the country and has little prospect of uniting it, ought not to be a candidate.

For however important the ideas for which he stands, he would be jeopardizing and not promoting them if they became involved in bitter class and sectional conflict.

Mr. Wallace's calling is that of a prophet. There is a wide difference between prophecy and government. As a prophet, and an agitator for his prophecies, Mr. Wallace has ranged far and wide. There is no doubt, I think, that there is in him much of the feeling and the tendency of things to come. But he is a mystic and isolated man to whom the shape of the real world is not clear, in which he is not at home and at ease. It is here, I believe, that the profound distrust of his being President originates, and I am speaking of those who like him and admire him and understand his ideas.

No one can be certain, of course, what responsibility will do to a man. It changes all men. But the politicians have to judge Mr. Wallace by assuming that he would be in the White House what he is in the Vice-Presidency. Many of the voters, too many to be disregarded, would feel, I think that his elevation to the Presidency would produce a profound, perhaps an unreasonable, sense of anxiety, and of loss of confidence in the conduct of the government.

This would arise, I think, not because Mr. Wallace is not a good man. On the contrary, he is an exceptionally fine human being. It would arise from an intuitive realization that his goodness is unworldly, that his heart is so detached from the realities that he has never learned to measure, as a statesman must, the relation of good and of evil in current affairs.

July 11, 1944

This column ran shortly before President Roosevelt let it be known that he did not want Wallace as his running mate in 1944. It makes a characteristic Lippmann distinction between a "good man" and the right man for the job. In 1945, Wallace was forced to resign as President Truman's Secretary of Commerce, after criti-cizing the administration's hard line on Russia. Although Wallace's bid for the Presidency in 1948 as candidate of the Progressive party did not have Lippmann's support, Wallace's views on the hazards of Cold War were not dissimilar to Lippmann's.

[*G.A.H.*]

Alfred Smith

Those who knew him best admire Al Smith the most, and all would wish if they could to perpetuate his fame. They cannot do this in the ordinary way by erecting a monument to some manifest public achievement with which his name will always be identified. For the greatness of Al Smith was that of the great performer—of the artist who acts his part, who plays his instrument, better than his audience have ever heard it done before. When the show is over, there is no record except in their own memories to prove his excellence, and only their personal testimony remains.

The stage on which he played his part was not the nation and not the world but the City and the State of New York. On that local stage he was, I shall always believe, the foremost master in our time of the art of popular government. He did not contend with the greatest issues of this epoch: he governed only one state of the Union during an interval in the 1920's of relative quiet and ease. But though he dealt with issues that few now remember, the way in which he dealt with them left an impress upon those who watched him and followed him that they do not forget.

When we try to define his peculiar distinction, we may say, I think, that he made good government popular in New York. That calls for rare gifts in any democracy. For the business of governing, when you really settle down to it, is over long stretches prosaic and tedious. To a degree which threatens the maintenance of democratic institutions, politicians who must appeal to masses of the voters make their living by talking about almost everything but the business of governing. Even in war time most political oratory has about as much relation to the conduct of the war and the making of peace as the radio plugs for laxatives, deodorants, and hair tonics have to the news of the day.

The greatest menace to popular government lies in this separation between what responsible officials have to do when they administer the government and what politicians talk about when they appeal for votes. For this means that democratic institutions are not educating the people for the tasks of government. While Al Smith was Governor of New York, he bridged this chasm as no one before or since has ever bridged it. He was able to fascinate great audiences with the business of financing and administering public affairs, and to make them share his own interest in problems that the ordinary public relations expert would say were too dull and over the people's heads.

It would be easy to think that he did this because he was such an engaging and amusing human being, and such a good showman. But that would be, I think, to miss the main point, which is that Al Smith knew the city and state like the palm of his hand: he knew the City Hall and the Legislature, and all the men who had been in them, and the institutions in every part of the state, and who was the head man and who was the janitor. When he thought about the public business, he was not thinking about a mass of boring papers on his desk at Albany but about the living persons and objects that went to make up the business of government.

His mastery of the subject was his real stock in trade: no one who heard him had the least doubt that he knew what he was talking about. There lay the difference between Al Smith and others who also in their own way had popular magic and a catchy style. He stood out above all the other showmen, and grew in popular confidence while they declined, because his were the honest goods, and the people, if they are given long enough to realize it and to choose, do in fact see through the charlatans.

His career is a standing contradiction to the notion, now so current, that experts in public relations can create a synthetic public man, that professionals can be hired to write speeches which will endow him with a fictitious personality, and make him seem to be what he is not. Al Smith was his own public relations expert as every first-rate public man has to be in the field, however large or small, where he works. The notion never entered his head that some one who was not running for office, who had not been elected to office, who had never walked the floor at night worrying over its responsibilities, could be his conscience, his brain and his voice. He would have said, I am sure, that the man who could do that for him ought to be the Governor of New York. For "public relations"

157

is another name for political leadership, the one function of a chief executive that it is impossible to delegate.

Al Smith's speeches were prepared in conversations with his kitchen Cabinet, and by cross-examining those who had expert knowledge. But no ghost wrote his speech. When he had got all the advice and the suggestions he wanted, he jotted down on an envelope the points he wished to cover, and then he went out before the audience and made, not read, a speech. No one can do that who is not so full of his subject that he has more to say than he has time to say, and is so sure of his knowledge that he is not afraid of making boners. But the effect was convincing in a way that no speech can be which the audience feels intuitively was written by some one who may have known more about the subject than the man who is reading it.

I do not suppose that this conveys much to those who did not know Al Smith when he was at the peak of his powers. For it is not easy to put into words a quality so indefinable, yet so overwhelmingly impressive when you meet it, as his luminous gift of mind and heart for making government altogether sincere in its contact with the people.

October 7, 1944

A graduate of the Fulton Street fish market on the Lower East Side of New York, speaker of the New York State Assembly, Sheriff of New York County, president of the City Board of Aldermen, and four-time governor of New York, Alfred E. Smith seemed an unlikely Lippmann hero. But he was. Smith's losing campaign for the Presidency against Herbert Hoover in 1928 was not helped by Smith's big city image, his Roman Catholicism, his opposition to Prohibition, and national prosperity.

[G.A.H.]

Harry Hopkins

If in one room some one had assembled say the twenty men, chiefs of state, foreign ministers, and high commanders, who organized the allied victory, and in another room an equal number of private citizens—if each group had then been asked to describe Harry Hopkins, an inquiring observer would not have believed they were talking about the same man.

There is a reason for this. The career of Harry Hopkins was divided into two chapters, one before May, 1940, when Hitler broke into Western Europe and reached the shores of the Atlantic, and one after. In the first chapter, that of the domestic New Deal, Harry Hopkins was on public view and his public reputation became fixed. In the second chapter, that of the war, he disappeared entirely from the public view, and in this vacuum of information his former reputation clung to him like a tin can to a dog's tail. Except among the relatively few who were planning and directing the war, Harry Hopkins was judged as a New Dealer. He was liked or disliked, suspected or trusted, not for what he was actually doing but for what he had done in the years before May, 1940.

His great work, upon which his lasting fame will rest, was done as the principal adviser and agent of President Roosevelt in the formation of the allied coalition. Through him, more than through any other American, the negotiations were conducted which produced the common strategical plan and the combined operations. That was his mission, whether he was administering lend-lease, or traveling back and forth among the capitals, or attending the councils of war in Washington, Casablanca, Cairo, Tehran, Quebec, Yalta, or working for the President with the combined and the joint chiefs of staff, or with the shipping, production, and resources boards.

No one would say that he was the inventor of the conception of a unified effort under a common strategical plan. But his contribution in making the conception workable was very great indeed. That is why his private reputation rose so high among those who knew most intimately what was going on, how great were the difficulties of collaboration, in the inner councils of the war. Even the outside observer, if he watched closely and was reasonably well informed, could detect an objective measure of his influence. There were alternating periods of decision and co-operation on the one hand, of hesitation and conflict on the other. These periods coincided remarkably, one began to see, with the periods when Harry Hopkins was active and in good health and with the periods when he was away from Washington or was ill.

Coalition warfare is notoriously difficult, and the coalition which won the second world war was the most complex, and also the most brilliantly successful, which statesmen and soldiers have ever organized. The coalition of the first world war was simple in comparison: moreover, it fell apart, as this one never did, before the war was concluded. The Napoleonic wars lasted for twenty years as one coalition after another dissolved.

We are too close to our own times to appreciate now the greatness of the achievement in uniting so many diverse nations in such gigantic campaigns all interlocked one with the other in every continent and on all the oceans. But the historians who write for our descendants will appreciate it, and the men who played a leading part in it, not least among them Harry Hopkins, will have a fame that is secure.

Of the personal qualities which enabled him to play his part, I would single out his lucidity and his fearlessness. They were, I think, two aspects of the same thing. He had what old Holmes, the justice, liked to call an instinct for the jugular, the gift of penetration, the knack of cutting aside the details and coming to the crux of the matter, of finding swiftly the real issue which had to be decided, the sticking point at which pride, vested interest, timidity, confusion, were causing trouble.

He would bring it nakedly into the open, ruthlessly, almost cynically, with no palaver, often with deliberate tactlessness meant to shock men into seeing the reality. These are not the qualities which make a conventionally successful politician. But in the grim business of war, among men who carry the tremendous burdens of decision, they were just the qualities which the times called for.

So fearless a mind does not exist except where there is also a fearless heart. After May, 1940, certainly, Harry Hopkins had come beyond all fear. He knew what the war meant, that unless it was won, life would not be worth living. He knew, too, I have no doubt, that he had not long to live. Yet by a chance, which always seemed to him curious, he found himself in one of the high places of the world at the most critical moment of its history.

Though he was not given to being grandiose about it, he did in fact then spend himself utterly, and he was indeed a dedicated man. Fearing nothing, he was uninhibited and could be perfectly lucid at least with himself, and as direct and penetrating in his advice and in negotiation as the traffic would bear.

Would there had been more like him. For his work was confined to the highest and most central issue of the war: the secondary and peripheral issues, which now rise to plague us, and the preparation of what was to be done with victory, he had little part in. For the President's health and his own had failed before they could take them in hand.

January 31, 1946

In poor health, Hopkins retired from government service about a year before his death. As FDR's administrator of the Federal Relief Administration in the 1930s, Hopkins had been called "the world's greatest spender." An intimate advisor of Roosevelt and his personal envoy on many overseas assignments, he played a role comparable to that of Colonel House in the Wilson administration.

[G.A.H.]

Mahatma Gandhi

In the life and death of Mahatma Gandhi we have seen re-enacted in our time the supreme drama of humanity. Gandhi was a political leader and he was a seer, and perhaps never before on so grand a scale has any one sought to shape the course of events in the world as it is by the example of a spirit which was not of the world as it is.

Gandhi was, as St. Paul said, transformed in the renewing of his mind, he was not "conformed to this world." Yet he sought to govern turbulent masses of men who were still very much conformed to this world, and have not been transformed. He died by violence as he was staking his life in order to set the example of non-violence.

Thus he posed again the perennial question of how the insight of the seers and saints is related to the work of legislators, rulers, and statesmen. That they are in conflict is only too plain, and yet it is impossible to admit, as Gandhi refused to admit, that the conflict can never be resolved. For it is necessary to govern mankind and it is necessary to transform men.

Perhaps we may say that the insight of the governors of men is, as it were, horizontal: They act in the present, with men as they are, with the knowledge they possess, with what they can now understand, with the mixture of their passions, and desires and instincts. They must work with concrete and with the plainly and generally intelligible things.

The insight of the seers, on the contrary, is vertical: They deal, however wide their appeal, with each person potentially, as he might be transformed, renewed, and regenerated. And because they appeal to experience which men have not yet had, with things that are not at hand and are out of their immediate reach, with the invisible and the unattained, they speak and act, as Gandhi did, obscurely, appealing to the imagination by symbolic evocation and subtle example.

The ideals of human life which the seers teach—non-resistance, humility, and poverty and chastity—have never been and can never be the laws of a secular society. Chastity, consistently and habitually observed, would annihilate it. Poverty, if universally pursued, would plunge it into misery and disease. Humility and non-resistance, if they were the rule, would mean the triumph of predatory force.

Is it possible that the greatest seers and teachers did not know this, and that what they enjoined upon men was a kind of suicide and self-annihilation? Obviously not. Their wisdom was not naive, and it can be understood if we approach it not as rules of conduct but as an insight into the economy and the order and the quality of the passions.

At the summit of their wisdom what they teach is, I think, not how in the practical issues of daily life men in society can and should behave, but to what ultimate values they should give their allegiance. Thus the injunction to render unto Caesar the things that are Caesar's is not a definite political principle which can be applied to define the relation of Church and State. It is an injunction as to where men shall have their ultimate obligations, that in rendering to Caesar the things that are Caesar's, they should not give to Caesar their ultimate loyalty, but should reserve it.

In the same manner to have humility is to have in the last reaches of conviction, a saving doubt. To embrace poverty is to be without possessiveness and a total attachment to things and to honors. To be non-resistant is to be at last non-competitive.

What the seer points toward is best described in the language of St. Paul as the creation of the new man. "And that ye put on the new man, which after God is created in righteousness and true holiness." What is this new man? He is the man who has been renewed and is "no longer under a schoolmaster," whose passions have been altered, as Gandhi sought to alter the passions of his countrymen, so that they need no discipline from without because they have been transformed from within. Such regenerated men can, as Confucius said, follow what their hearts desire without transgressing what is right. They are "Led of the spirit" in the Pauline language, and therefore they "are not under the law."

It is not for such men as them that governments are instituted and laws enacted and enforced. These are for the old Adam. It is for the aggressive, possessive, carnal appetites of the old Adam that there are punishments and rewards, and for his violence a superior force.

It is only for the regenerate man, whose passions have been transformed, that the discipline of the law and of power are no longer needed, nor any incentive or reward beyond the exquisite and exhilarating wholesomeness and unity and freedom of his own passions.

February 3, 1948

Harold Ickes

In his later years, which was when I came to know him personally, Harold Ickes would often be tired and depressed until he had incited himself to righteous indignation at some new instance of corruption or cowardice. Then he would be ageless, young again from the lust of battle, and the evening would be a success. At first I used to think that he was like an old fire horse who would waste away and die unless at least once a day somebody rang the fire alarm. Once I said that to him just to see him rear up.

But after a while I came to know better. It was true that a good quarrel was as necessary to him as food and drink. It was true that he was the greatest living master of the art of quarreling. And like all men who have mastered an art, he was proud of it and liked to practice it, and to show it off. But it was not true, as he liked to pretend, that he was quarrelsome because he was bad-tempered. He was a kind and generous and warm-hearted man.

The Old Curmudgeon business was a false front to protect him against its being generally realized how violently virtuous, how furiously righteous, how angrily unbigoted he was almost all the time. He was aware, having lived long and truly, how boring virtue can be made to seem, how unsufferable would be his high-mindedness if it were served up neat.

Thus he took pains to be righteous and interesting too.

Then I learned to appreciate the special quality of his honesty and of his courage. I do not know how to begin to describe them except to say that he had a patrician's sense, a patrician's certainty that he was a proprietor in the nation's estate, and that it belonged to him in essentially the same way as did his private estate. A grafter was not a man who had swindled the great, impersonal, bureaucratic government; a grafter was the contemptible, degenerate son who had swindled his father. The public property belonged to the people, of whom he was one, as his watch and his wallet belonged to him, and no one could pick his pockets and walk away unmolested.

This is not a code of ethics which men observe because they must, because they may be investigated, because they may be put in prison, in so far as they cannot get away with something and around the code. His was the noble way where virtue is the man's own inner self.

There courage is as natural as honesty, and they are in fact identical and inseparable. The reason why Harold Ickes was never afraid to say what he thought was that it would never have occurred to him that any man would dare to question his patriotism, his loyalty, and his honor. Whose country was this if it was not Harold Ickes's country? And who was the little faker who could dare to pretend that he was more loyal to and more concerned with this country than was Harold Ickes—who owned it? No one ever dared to take him on where his honor was involved. It would have been like asking Winston Churchill whether he was in fact an Englishman and competent to judge what it was loyal and patriotic for an Englishman to be or to think.

Thus Harold Ickes could fight well, being altogether invulnerable within himself.

It is almost unnecessary to add that though he spent his life as a reformer and a progressive and, in his own special version of it, as a New Dealer, he was an unqualified American fundamentalist. To him all the things against which he fought, graft, monopoly, bigotry, were crimes and rebellions against the true American system. He did not think of himself, therefore, as engaged in making a new and different, and supposedly better world. His character and his philosophy had become firm long before the modern planners and collectivists appeared, and for a while took over the cause of reform and of progress and even of liberalism.

His great quarrels were to defend, to restore, to recover property and rights that had always belonged to Americans. And I have no doubt that even when he seemed for a moment to be alone, he never felt that he was alone. For he was perfectly sure, I believe, that in the battle he was one of the invisible hosts of the American dead and of the Americans who are not yet born.

February 7, 1952

The nation's natural resources had no fiercer watchdog than "Honest Harold." After many threats to do so, he resigned as Secretary of the Interior in 1946, when President Truman proposed appointing a California oil tycoon (and generous contributor to the Democratic party) to a job Ickes thought he shouldn't have. Ickes and Lippmann shared an early enthusiasm for the "Bull Moosers" who rallied around Theodore Roosevelt and the Progressive party in 1912.

[*G.A.H.*]

Charles de Gaulle

Having been one of his American admirers since June of 1940, when he raised his flag in Britain and summoned the French to go on with the war, I cannot pretend to write dispassionately about Gen. de Gaulle. But now that he is coming back to Washington in triumph, I have been asking myself what is the secret of this famous man?

The secret is that he is more than a great man. He is a great man in the sense that he has taken a great part in historic events. But there were other great men in the war days. In addition to being an historic man, he is also, which is rarer than greatness, a genius. This is the special quality which he, and I think only he, shares with Churchill.

His genius consists in the capacity to see beneath the surface of events, to see through the obvious and conventional and stereotyped appearance of events to the significant realities, to the obscured facts and forces which will prevail. This gift, which is more than leadership as such, is second sight into the nature of history. It brings with it the gift of prophesying what is going to happen because to the seeing eye it is already there.

The ability to see truly the significant reality carries with it the ability to convey what his vision brings him. Men like Churchill and de Gaulle do not sign ghost-written books and they do not read ghost-written speeches. For the vision is their own and they alone can communicate it.

Thus, in the bitter days of 1940 when France had fallen and Britain stood alone, it called for a great man, for a brave man, for a resolute and faithful man, to go into exile and from there to organize the French resistance. But it took genius to see how this noble but desperate venture would end, and to see that France, defeated, demoralized and prostrate, remained one of the great pow-

168

ers, to see that in the end she would be—as is now the fact—among the principal shapers of the settlement with Germany.

Thinking of all that has happened in these twenty years, it occurred to me to see whether or not my memory was deceiving me. Was it true, as ever since I have believed, that in the darkest days of the most desperate of modern wars, Gen. de Gaulle had communicated his vision of an enduring and an undefeated France?

I find that about three weeks after the fall of France, I had learned enough to be able to write that "in the misfortune of France it should be our fierce pride to be the last to forget the greatness of France. We must wish to be the first to remember . . . that France is indispensable, as indispensable to the maturity of Western civilization as Hellas was to its birth—and as imperishable."

I learned to say that only from Gen. de Gaulle.

April 21, 1960

Dag Hammarskjold

Over the years I have often wondered whether Dag Hammarskjold [Second Secretary-General of the United Nations, killed in a plane crash in the Congo, September 17, 1961] belonged to an age that is passing or to one that is being born. He was a bold innovator in world affairs, and he opened up a future, having carried further than it has ever been carried before the principle of international action to promote peace. Yet he was himself the fine flower of the European tradition of civility which, if it is not dying, certainly is not flourishing today.

He was altogether not the mass man of our times. He could be a very good friend but there was a deep reserve in his character which few if any can have penetrated. In the great public world where the white lights blazed upon him, he lived an inner life of contemplation and esthetic experience that had nothing to do with power and popularity and publicity. His diplomacy had a finesse and a courtliness in the great traditions of Europe. Never before, and perhaps never again, has any man used the intense art of diplomacy for such unconventional and such novel experiments.

The biggest experiment, for which in the end he gave his life, was to move the international society of the United Nations from having to choose between a very difficult police action in Korea and sole reliance on debate and verbal expression. He moved the UN onto the plane of executive action without large-scale war as in Korea. This movement from words to deeds, from general resolutions to intervention, was best seen during the crisis at Suez, in Palestine, in Laos, and then in the enormous, the infinitely difficult and the infinitely dangerous crisis in the Congo.

I knew Dag Hammarskjold long enough and well enough, I think, to understand why he accepted the risks of opening up new paths in such wild and uncharted country. He was not an innovator because he had an itch to change things. He was a political inovator because there was no decent alternative. He saw no alternative to intervention by the United Nations in a crisis where there was a bitter confrontation in the cold war.

No cautious and timid man would have dreamed of staking the prestige and perhaps the future of the United Nations, as well as his personal reputation and his office, on the attempt to pacify the Congo. But great as were the risks of intervention, the risks of letting events run their course were much greater. If the United Nations now fails in what Hammarskjold inaugurated, the prospects are that the terrible racial struggle between Europeans and Africans will become deeply entangled in the conflict between the Western Powers and the Communist Powers of the Soviet Union and China.

It was to avert and to prevent this fatal entanglement that Hammarskjold dared to use the powers of the United Nations. The outcome is as yet unknown. But what we do know is that his unprecedented innovation in world affairs has run into fearful resistance both in the East and in the West. Hammarskjold's use of the UN to isolate and disinfect the Congo crisis brought on him and the UN the implacable hatred of the Soviet government. At the same time Hammarskjold did not have the full support of the Western Powers. In Algeria, in Katanga, in Angola, in Rhodesia, and in South Africa there is bitter resistance to the objectives of the United Nations in the Congo. Those objectives are to protect the transition from white supremacy, which cannot be continued much longer, to African self-government for which the Africans are so unprepared.

There is no doubt that in the administration of the new UN policy there have been mistakes, errors of judgment and failures of personnel. But let us keep it in mind that the cause of the two-sided opposition to the UN action is not the mistakes, which are not irreparable. The cause of the opposition from East and West is a determination not to have the UN succeed in what it is attempting to do. For if the UN succeeds, there will not be a Communist government in the Congo. That is what Khrushchev hates about Hammarskjold and the Secretary General's Office. And if the UN succeeds, there will not be a restoration of white supremacy in the Congo, and that is why money, propaganda and clandestine intervention are being employed to frustrate the UN.

171

No one knows today who can come after Hammarskjold, and there are many signs that he is in fact irreplaceable. For Hammarskjold was made Secretary General at a time when the UN was really no more than a debating society. Except for the police action in Korea it passed resolutions which aimed at mediation and conciliation, but it did not in any important place command executive action.

It is easy to say that the world is not ready for international action to establish peace, and it would be hard to refute such a statement. Hammarskjold, under the fearful pressure of circumstances, resorted to international action. With his extraordinary diplomatic elegance and finesse, he used successfully international action at Suez, in Palestine, and in Laos. As compared with these the Congo presented a new order of difficulty, and the outcome, now that Hammarskjold is dead, is in the gravest doubt.

If the world is not ready for what Hammarskjold felt compelled to try in the Congo, it is also true, I hate to say, that this present world is not ready for the kind of man Hammarskjold was. He was a Western man in the highest traditions of political excellence in the West. Khrushchev says that Hammarskjold was not neutral in the Congo, and that there is no such thing as a neutral man. Hammarskjold was in fact the embodiment of the noblest Western political achievement—that laws can be administered by judges and civil servants who have their first allegiance to the laws, and not to their personal, their class or even their national interests.

No such political ideal is believed to be possible or is regarded as tolerable in the Marxist world. The ideal is not very well understood in most of the rest of the world, and there is no use pretending that such public servants are not very rare indeed. So there are times, as now in this hour of our grief and shock, when the ideal seems to belong to things that are passing away.

September 21, 1961

J. William Fulbright

The Arkansas senatorial campaign will bring a confrontation between traditional American conservatism and a wholly new phenomenon, a radical reaction sailing under the flag of conservatism. This reactionary radicalism has as little relation to conservatism as the so-called peoples' democracies beyond the Iron Curtain have to democracy.

The true conservatives, of whom the greatest in this century is Churchill, are indissolubly at one with the constitutional sources of the nation's life. For them the nation is a living thing which grows and changes, and they think of themselves as participating in this growth and change. Because they themselves are so secure and certain about what is essential and fundamental, the most intelligent conservatives are liberal in temper and progressive in policy.

Sen. Fulbright is that kind of conservative, and so he is a standing challenge to the reactionary radicals who are in revolt against all the main developments of the twentieth century.

They are against the consequences of modern science and technology which have brought into being a concentration of masses of people in cities, masses of people uprooted from their ancestral ways of life. These radical reactionaries are against the welfare state which provides these urban masses with some of that personal security which their ancestors in the country made in their communities. And they are against the regulation of this enormously complex economy, though without regulation it would churn itself up into crisis and chaos.

The reactionary radicals, who would like to repeal the twentieth century, are, so they tell us, violently opposed to communism. But communism also belongs to the twentieth century and these reactionary radicals do not understand it and do not know how to

173

resist it. Thus they do not want the alliances with which we have contained communism in Europe at the armistice lines of World War II. They are against foreign aid which is used to help new countries and weak countries help themselves without succumbing to communism. They despise the United Nations which has so much to do in opening up for the new and inexperienced countries the roads to freedom. They do believe loyally in American military power. But they do not understand it. They do not understand that the United States, though very strong, is not omnipotent, and that we cannot set the world in order and achieve total victory over communism by issuing ultimata. Their irresponsibility in foreign affairs is such that if the President did for the country what they say he ought to be doing, there would be going on at one and the same time another Korean War in Southeast Asia, a somewhat smaller Algerian war in Cuba, and a thermo-nuclear war about Berlin.

Sen. Fulbright, with the authority and with the intimate knowledge that come to him as chairman of the Foreign Relations Committee of the Senate, has stood firmly against such irresponsible nonsense. The nation is greatly in his debt. The role he plays in Washington is an indispensable role. There is no one else who is so powerful and also so wise, and if there were any question of removing him from public life, it would be a national calamity.

Not only has he been the bravest and wisest of advisers. He is also the most farseeing and constructive. It has been said of him that all too often he has been right too soon. That is a great compliment. In our democracy somebody who is listened to must be right before it is popular to be right. Here Sen. Fulbright has a distinguished record which goes back to the second world war when, still an unknown and unnoticed Congressman from Arkansas, he brought out the Fulbright resolution which led the change of American opinion against isolation.

He was, I think, the first American public man who realized that if Western Europe was to coexist with the Soviet Union, it would have to unite. And he is the first responsible American statesman to be saying that the necessary counterweight to the development of the Communist power is a much closer political and economic integration of the Western World.

October 12, 1961

174

Fulbright won this campaign and was re-elected to the Senate in 1968, but to Lippmann's regret was defeated the next time around, in 1974. Lippmann's high regard for the Senator increased in the mid-1960s when Fulbright, as chairman of the Foreign Relations Committee, urged American military withdrawal from Indochina.

[*G.A.H.*]

Pope John XXIII

The reign of Pope John has been a wonder which grows more astounding the more we think how amidst the angry enmities of our time he became so greatly loved. It is a modern miracle that anyone could reach across all the barriers of class, caste, color and creed to touch the hearts of all kinds of people. There has been nothing like it, certainly not in the modern age. The miracle is a proof which we sorely needed that all the varieties of men do actually belong to one human family. Otherwise, so many could not have heard and understood and responded to Pope John.

That they have responded is proof that the enmities and divisions of mankind are not the whole reality of the human condition. There is in men a capacity, unplumbed and perhaps unmeasurable, to be reached by loving kindness. The miracle of Pope John is that he knew this and believed it and had faith to act upon it, and that he was proved to have been right. So, as he lies dead, he is revered and blessed by all sorts and conditions of men all around the globe.

We know that the miracle of Pope John will not transform the world. The condition of man is a hard one, and his struggle to survive and to prevail will not disappear with the appearance of a saint and the proclamation of a saving truth. We shall not suddenly become new men. But the universal response which Pope John evoked is witness to the truth that there is in the human person, however prone to evil, an aptitude for goodness. That is why we must never despair that the world can be better than the world we live in.

It is evident to anyone who reads the two great encyclical letters, "Mater et Magistra" ("Mother and Teacher") and "Pacem in Terris" ("Peace on Earth"), that Pope John, far from being naive and unworldly, had an encyclopædic and acute knowledge of the complex and stubborn problems of the daylight world. The encyclical letters do not suppose that the world can be cured before the problems that harass it are brought to solution. The encyclical letters are, therefore, directed to the solution of human problems of ordinary men. They are cornerstones of an imposing construction which, as it is carried forward, will become acceptable and increasingly self-evident to men who deal toward each other with respect for the human person and for his reason.

The belief that there are such self-evident concepts and propositions has been denied by many in the modern age. Yet our own American institutions were founded by men who had been taught to think it self-evident that men are capable of reason and that this is a universe which can be lived in rationally. The Founding Fathers inherited this belief. For modern secular men, who have been taught to reject it, an act of faith is needed. When the belief exists, as it did so profoundly in Pope John, it can become the intellectual core of what can be a human doctrine which transcends conflicting diversity.

The movement to bring the teachings of the Church to bear upon "the process of radical change" in the modern "economic and political situation" begins, says Pope John, with Pope Leo XIII. The first of the great modernizing social messages is the encyclical "Rerum Novarum" of May 15, 1891, on "The Condition of the Working Classes." Pope John carried forward this movement not only in his two great encyclical letters but by calling together the Ecumenical Council.

What will now come of all this will be of critical importance not only to the Catholic Church but to all churches and to all governments. In any event, the modernizing movement can perhaps be arrested but it cannot for long be turned back. For what Pope John began will have very big consequences, and the history of our world will be different because he lived.

June 6, 1963

Herbert Hoover

It is hard to recapture for those who did not know Herbert Hoover during the First World War the brilliance of his reputation and the personal fascination of the man.

The Nation had entered the war reluctantly and resentfully. The American people were predominantly isolationist, believing that our ramparts were the two oceans, and they were pacifists and they hated war. Hoover, though he was a Quaker and at heart a conscientious objector to war, had in fact intervened spectacularly long before Woodrow Wilson felt himself forced to ask Congress for a declaration of war. Hoover had intervened by the gallant enterprise of saving the Belgian people during the German occupation. This struck a deep response in a nation which realized that neutrality was inglorious and probably impossible but yet recoiled at the butchery.

When this country entered the war, Hoover was already a legendary figure. He was also an entrancing talker. Many felt, as I did, that they had never met a more interesting man, anyone who knew so much of the world and could expound so clearly what to almost all Americans in 1917 were the inscrutable mysteries of European politics.

When the war ended in 1918 and the presidential election of 1920 began to take shape, Hoover was the first choice of nearly all the Wilsonian idealists, of the progressives and liberals in both parties. Destiny had marked him, I have always thought, to be the natural heir of Woodrow Wilson, and in fact he was launched into national politics by men who belonged to Wilson's following. He chose, however, to declare himself a Republican, and this decision, which brought him to the Presidency eight years later, opened up a breach with the progressives and liberals. It was deepened and envenomed by the 1932 campaign, and it was not until much later

178

in his life that the breach was healed, thanks to the initiative of President Truman.

At a time like this, it would be foolish to attempt to anticipate the verdict of history. Those of us who knew Hoover during his public career may, perhaps, allow themselves a few reflections. I would venture to say that for the disaster which engulfed him in the White House Hoover was in no way responsible. In the 1920s when the Great Depression was brewing, there was no one, no politician or financier, who had any clear idea as to how the world should be reconstructed after a devastating war. It was then normal, though almost no one remembered it, that in modern history a great war is followed by a great crash.

We avoided such a crash after the Second World War because we had so well learned the lessons of the First World War. So far as I knew, Hoover himself never accepted the tenets of the modern school of monetary and fiscal management which are applied in all advanced countries today.

But it's an interesting historical fact that as President he adopted pragmatically virtually all the main principles of the early years of Roosevelt's New Deal. The reader will find the basic text for this assertion in Hoover's speech accepting the Republican nomination on August 11, 1932. Writing three years later in the light of the unfolding New Deal program, I ventured to say that Hoover's

historic position as a radical innovator has been greatly underestimated and . . . Mr. Roosevelt's pioneering has been greatly exaggerated. It was Mr. Hoover who abandoned the principles of laissez faire in relation to the business cycle, established the conviction that prosperity and depression can be publicly controlled by political action, and drove out of the public consciousness the old idea that depressions must be overcome by private adjustment.

In the 1932 speech of acceptance, Mr. Hoover said that "the function of the Federal Government in these times is to use its reserve powers and its strength for the protection of citizens and local government by support to our institutions against forces beyond their control." Hoover's recovery program included a deliberate policy of inflating the base of credit, the use of government credit to supplement the deficiency of private credit, reduction of

179

the normal expenses of government but an increase of the extraordinary expenditures—the expansion of public works in order to create employment; the assumption by the Federal Government of the ultimate responsibility for relief of destitution where local or private resources were inadequate. This increase was not to be covered by taxation but by deficit financing.

While Hoover is remembered now as a great objector to the course of affairs since 1932, this was, I believe, the effect of his disastrous accident in 1929—his being run over by the Great Depression. His negativism was not in harmony with his generous, liberal, and magnanimous nature.

In the field of war and peace, however, Herbert Hoover remained true to his original nature, that of the bold and brilliant philanthropist who binds up wounds and avoids inflicting them. Hoover fed the defeated Germans, and though he hated communism, he fed the Bolsheviks. Yet in spite of all of it he never believed in America as a global power with military and political commitments in every continent. He was an isolationist and, insofar as his beliefs could be reconciled with his duties as President and Commander in Chief, he was a conscientious objector.

I remember him affectionately. Thus, in 1928 when he was nominated for President, I sent him congratulations and good wishes. He replied to me at my office in the *New York World,* which was supporting Governor Smith, that "I do not expect you to love me publicly until after November."

October 22, 1964

Although Lippmann sent "congratulations and best wishes" to the Great Engineer, he backed Hoover's unsuccessful opponent, Al Smith.

[G.A.H.]

180

Adlai Stevenson

Adlai Stevenson was not a common man or a typical American of our times or, indeed, of any other time. But he evoked for us the mystic chords of memory because he touched again "the better angels of our nature." From Lincoln to Adlai Stevenson the heritage is direct and unbroken, a family tradition which began with his great-grandfather. Like Lincoln he made men feel what this Nation had to be if the American experiment was to succeed. Like Lincoln he was what the prairies and the New World had made of the educated Englishmen who led this country in the 18th Century.

This Lincolnian American is, as compared with Washington or Jefferson, the first authentic American, the new man of the New World. Before Lincoln, the distinguished Americans were transplanted Englishmen. Since Lincoln there has existed the idea of a special American type which is excellent and admirable and holds the promise of a better human future. Adlai Stevenson was a rare, perhaps a late-blooming, example of such an American. He was admired by the discerning all over the world and greatly loved. An essential ingredient of the admiration and the love was the knowledge that only America could have produced him, and that this revealed what America really was.

The question is now whether this country is still devoted to the American idea which he embodied. No one supposes, of course, that the country can be filled with Stevensons any more than a hundred years ago it was filled with Lincolns, any more than Britain is filled with Churchills. It is only occasionally and for a while that nations are represented by their greater men. The question is whether in our critical moments the better angels of our nature respond to our authentic ideals.

For there is abroad in this land today a very different spirit con-

181

tending for the soul of our people. The original American has had for a central idea, as Lincoln said at Gettysburg, that America was an experiment of consequence to all mankind and that, primarily, the influence of America was its example. The new spirit among us is measured by our money and our power.

The struggle between the two spirits has appeared and reappeared throughout our history. But with the enormous and sudden increase of our power and wealth, the stress and strain of the struggle for the American soul has become fierce. It is the uncertainty as to which spirit will prevail that divides, more than tactics or manners or policy, the American people among themselves and from the world around us.

Adlai Stevenson's enemies were not men whom he had injured. He injured no men. His enemies were men who recognized that he did not share and was a living reproach to the new imperiousness of our power and wealth, that he was a deeply established American who had no part in the arrogance of the newly rich and the newly powerful and the newly arrived. His very presence made them uncomfortable, even abashed all the more because he was so witty when they were so hot, so elegant when they were making a spectacle of themselves.

Shall we see his like again? Or was he the last of his noble breed? On this question hangs the American future. On one course we shall plunge ourselves into the making of a ramshackle empire in an era when no empire can long survive, and we shall wave the flag to cover our spiritual nakedness.

Or, we shall, as Adlai Stevenson would have done, remain true to our original loyalty, and transcending assertiveness, vulgar ambition, and the seductions of power, we shall make this country not only great and free but at peace with its own conscience.

July 20, 1965

After UN Ambassador Stevenson's sudden death in London, this tribute to "the last of his noble breed" was read with mixed feelings by Stevenson's friends, who had vainly urged Lippmann to endorse their candidate against General Eisenhower in 1952 and in 1956. In '52, Lippmann believed that only a moderate Republican administration could control Senator Joseph McCarthy and his hysterical hunt for "subversives" and could satisfactorily end the war in Korea.

[G.A.H.]

Konrad Adenauer

Adenauer can best be appreciated, I think, if we recognize him as first of all a Rhinelander. For he had only a perfunctory loyalty to the Germany of Bismarck and the Hohenzollerns. He was a Rhinelander in the sense that his deepest personal attachment was to the European lands which once lay within the frontiers of the Roman Empire. Thus he was, as so many have been saying, a passionate "European." But Europe for him did not really go beyond the Roman frontiers and did not include Eastern Europe. Nor, in fact, did Konrad Adenauer have a fervid attachment to Eastern Germany with its Protestant and Socialist majorities.

Therefore, Adenauer paid only lip service to the idea of German reunification. The allegiance to Roman Europe, which includes only a part of Europe and of Germany, defines his historic achievements. Adenauer is the man who rose out of the Hitler catastrophe to restore West Germany, to restore the self respect of the West Germans, to expiate the shame and disgrace of Hitler's Germany, and thus to restore respect again for the German name in the Western world. For this he will always be honored and gratefully remembered.

But while he achieved this much, the other side of him—his lack of sympathy for Eastern Europe—made him unable to see clearly into the future of Europe. His last great achievement in undoing the wrongs that Hitler had done was to make a peace of reconciliation between Western Germany and Gaullist France. But Adenauer did not see beyond that. Unlike General de Gaulle, who came to realize that the cold war had begun to thaw out, that Europe would have to be reunited "to the Urals," Adenauer was unable to acquire this prophetic vision.

As a result, a very considerable part of his foreign policy has been bypassed by events. Adenauer is the hero of the German rehabilitation but he is not the prophet of the German future.

What he did not see, what his friend and collaborator, [Secretary of State] John Foster Dulles did not see, was that the two Germanys could only be reunited in a larger Europe which did not end with the Elbe River.

Adenauer believed, as he once explained to me, reading from some intelligence reports, that Western Communist Europe was going to collapse, and that in the chaos, the Western powers would roll back the Red invasion and take hold once again of Poland and of the lands conquered by the Teutonic Knights. The policy of the rollback was the central belief in the days of the Adenauer-Dulles axis, and it was the only policy then regarded as acceptable for ending the cold war and reuniting Germany.

It failed totally, and no one in authority in any country believes in it. Western Germany today is in the hands of men who have turned their backs on Adenauer's East European policy.

Adenauer will be buried with honors, most justly so. He will be honored for what he did to right the wrongs that Hitler did to Western civilization. But he will not be looked upon as the guide and the prophet when men think about the future of Germany and Europe.

April 25, 1967

John F. Kennedy

In the years since John F. Kennedy was murdered, we have had a chance to see a legend in the making, and I, for one, have learned a new respect for the myth-making process. The popular legend treats him as the new man who, coming to power as the old order of things dissolved, foresaw the shape of things to come.

The prosaic documentary record of his life and his opinions and his deeds has to be read with the eye of the imagination to discern this legendary figure. But a passionate multitude all over the world believes him to have been the herald of better things in dangerous and difficult times.

The artistic energy which is creating the legend has taken hold of bits and pieces of what really happened to compose a picture of what the new generation of our century wishes desperately were happening—the whole truth about how men can live and how they can be governed. Yet the actuality of the Kennedy administration is a very mixed collection of errors and false starts and brilliant illuminations of the future.

Thus, in prosaic fact, President Kennedy's conduct of foreign relations was quite fumbling until a few months before he died. There was the fiasco of the Bay of Pigs. There was the fiasco of his first handling of European affairs, beginning with the misunderstanding and suspicions of the Vienna conversations with Khrushchev and going on to the miscalculation in which he was outwitted by the building of the Berlin Wall.

But the myth-making impulse has rightly passed over these mistakes and has reached out toward that period when, having played his cards so well in the second Cuban crisis, he was inspired to proclaim the beginning of the end of the cold war with the Soviet Union. The legend of Kennedy the peacemaker rests on what happened in the last few months of his life when he was inspired to

185

seize an opportunity which the course of history had offered him.

In our internal affairs his reputation rests not on his realistic accomplishments, for they were few and he was in a deadlock with Congress, but on the right choices he occasionally made. In his legend he will always be remembered, for example, as the president who first adopted the teachings of modern economics about the management of the business cycle. In point of fact he adopted them reluctantly and almost certainly with no great understanding of them.

He is identified also with what is becoming the vast enterprise of dealing with the remaking of the human environment, the adaptation of modern technology to man's needs. It would be hard to put together an imposing record of what he actually accomplished here. But there is the undeniable fact that a whole generation of thinkers and experts in these matters was inspired by him, and swear by him now.

I was not, myself, an original Kennedy man, and although I supported him in 1960, I was skeptical and often disappointed until the last few months of his life. But now, in retrospect, I am glad of the legend and I think it contains that part of the truth which is most worth having.

This is the conviction, for which he set the example, that a new age has begun and that men can become the masters of their fate.

November 22, 1967

John F. Kennedy went out of his way to win Lippmann's good will, but Lippmann remained aloof. He found it hard to forgive the son for the father, Joseph Kennedy, whom Lippmann had known. In the first lively months of the Kennedy administration, the exhilaration was contagious and Lippmann was touched by it, but his ultimate judgment was that "Kennedy was not that good."

[G.A.H.]

186

Eugene McCarthy

A cynic, wrote Oscar Wilde, is a man who knows the price of everything and the value of nothing. The cynics are having a hard time explaining Senator McCarthy's challenge to the renomination of President Johnson. For by ordinary, worldly, so-called pragmatic standards, it is impossible to promise that Senator McCarthy will be nominated or that he will lead the way to the nomination of Sen. Robert Kennedy, or that he will change the policies of the Johnson Administration, that he will end the war, or restore the Democratic Party to its '64 commitments.

But when we look beyond all this, we can see that there are at issue in the McCarthy campaign the deepest and most cherished values of American political life. McCarthy has come forward as the defender of the American faith. What he stands for is the avowal that the American system of party government shall not be held to be a fraud and a deception, that it is a valid way by which the mass of our people can redress their grievances, can express their will, and can participate in the government of the nation.

The true significance of McCarthy's appearance is that these fundamental American values are in serious danger. We are on the way to a massive disbelief and despair about our political system. It is no small service on his part to have raised a flag to which the dissenting and the despairing can repair because they see again a political way to express themselves. They do not have to win. In a democratic country everybody cannot always be a winner. But in a healthy democracy everybody can believe, even when he loses, that he has been honestly heard, has made himself felt, has had a fair chance to take part in the give-and-take of debate and of voting.

The worst side effect of the Vietnam war has been that among so many Americans, most especially among the downtrodden minority of our people, faith in the central principle of a free and democratic society has been badly hurt. The taking of drugs to forget it all, the idea that only violence and sabotage and irreconcilability have any effect, the great movement of withdrawal, the movement to nihilism, separatism and alienation, the hopelessness, the despair, the cynicism—all these are the symptoms of the disintegration of the central hope of American society.

The most serious accusation that can be laid against the Johnson Administration is that it has corrupted and undermined the faith of our people in their political system. We are paying a terrible price for the breaking of the promises made in 1964 and the working out secretly of the consequences of the breaking of those promises to which the voters, when President Johnson was a candidate in 1964, committed him. It has been very costly to break the bonds of good faith that ought to bind a President and his people.

The reversal of the pledges of 1964 has been carried forth by deception. The attempt has been made to keep the war as painless as possible to the civilians and as invisible as possible to the mass of the voters. No calling up of the reserves and no mobilization. Until recently and very late in the day, no taxes to pay for the war. Only reneging on the promises of internal reform. No genuine debate about the legality of the war, no genuine debate on the American interest in the war. A kaleidoscope of showpieces, like the Manila conference when promises were made that no serious person believes can be fulfilled.

All this is often called the credibility gap. But what it means is that the American political system is being so managed and so exploited that the young people, who have not yet settled down into complacency and cynicism, are outraged and are ceasing to believe that our political system is honorable and has a meaning.

The mission of Senator McCarthy is to do whatever a gifted and honest man can do to stop the rot in the American political system. His chief assets are his own profoundly educated belief in the American idea and, as the campaign will show, the sincerity and purity of his motives. I do not expect to see him unhorse Lyndon Johnson. I do not expect him to force a change in the policies to which President Johnson has now so irretrievably committed the Democratic Party. But Eugene McCarthy will have spoken out and there will have been close to him some new men who will in time pull the Democratic Party out of the disaster into which it has been led.

My own view is that under the American two-party system there is only one way in which the country can now be brought out of the despair in which it finds itself. There is need of another new deal. So I hold that it has become a national interest that the Johnson Democratic Party, as it is now led and controlled, be ousted by a rejuvenated Republican Party. This may not happen. But if it cannot happen, the country is in for very difficult, I fear for very bitter, times.

December 18, 1967

The rejuvenated Republican party Lippmann hoped would succeed the Johnson administration turned out to be a Nixon-led party which did not strenuously foster internal reform, or moderate growing domestic alienation and cynicism, or conduct a debate on the legality or wisdom of the U.S. military intervention in Indochina. The scholarly and witty Senator McCarthy of Minnesota, who agreed with Lippmann on these points, lost the Democratic Presidential nomination to Senator Hubert Humphrey, who supported Lyndon Johnson's war policy, and thereby forfeited Lippmann's sympathy.

[G.A.H.]